Crimson & Blue

HANDBOOK

Stories, Stats and Stuff About KU Basketball

By Eric Nelson and Lauretta McMillen
Design & Layout by Jeff Pulaski

First Printing December 1993
Second Printing January 1994
Third Printing October 1994

Printed in the United States of America by
Mennonite Press, Inc.

ISBN 1-880652-31-5

PHOTO CREDITS Photographs on pages 6-59
and on page 68 were provided by the
University Archives at the University of
Kansas. All other photographs are from the
files of the Wichita Eagle.

COLLEGIATE
LICENSED
PRODUCT ™

ACKNOWLEDGMENTS

As with any book, this one would not have been completed without the help of a number of people. Some need to be specifically recognized here. First, thanks to Bill Handy, the Wichita Eagle's director of development, who made this project possible. Also to Jeff Pulaski, the artist who designed the cover and the book and made us look good. And to Jeff Rush, who copyedited the whole thing and now knows more about Kansas basketball than any Michigan graduate cares to.

At the University of Kansas, we are especially thankful for the helpful staff at the University Archives at the Spencer Research Library in Lawrence. John Nugent, Barry Bunch and Ned Kehde spent hours helping us, put up with many bothersome requests and even cheered us on when the hours of looking at tiny type in old newspapers began to wear on us. The bulk of the photographs in the first four chapters come from the Archives' files, and the staff was invaluable in collecting them, getting prints made and making identifications wherever possible.

The "stories" and "stuff" in this book come mainly from old newspapers, yearbooks, magazines and photos, and we are obviously indebted to those writers and photographers who have followed the Jayhawks over the years. We especially found access to the University Daily Kansan library helpful.

Credit for the "stats" in this book must go to the award-winning Sports Information Department at the University of Kansas. All of the numbers, lists and records that appear in Chapter 8 come from the KU basketball media guide. Copy preparation for this chapter was done by Andrea Baker of the Eagle development department. In addition, the media guide was a valuable cross-reference for dozens of scores, season records and other facts.

Finally, thanks must go to those who are close to us and supported us in this effort. Most of them also are Jayhawk fans, and we look forward to getting reacquainted with them.

For my parents, Marlin and Deanna, and my sister, Karsten. Also for the boys (Kyle, Tory, Bret and Chad). – J.E.N.

For Jessica Mae, who was already learning the "Rock Chalk Chant" on her changing table at 6 months old. – L.M.

INTRODUCTION

For nearly a century, basketball has been an inescapable part of life at the University of Kansas. That's what happens when a school brings the inventor of the game to campus and then follows him with some of college basketball's most successful coaches. Dr. James Naismith. William Hamilton. Dr. F.C. "Phog" Allen. Dick Harp. Ted Owens. Larry Brown. And now, Roy Williams. Each has made considerable contributions to the rich history that is Jayhawk basketball.

Tradition. The Kansas basketball program positively drips with it. In this book, we've tried to bring some of that tradition together in one place. These pages obviously do not contain everything there is to know about KU basketball. Rather, as the title indicates, this book is a collection of "stories, stats and stuff" that we, as KU graduates and devoted Jayhawk fans ourselves, thought others might like to know.

We've presented it in a format we hope you'll find comfortable. Because there have been only seven coaches, we divided the book according to their tenures. (In Phog Allen's case, his chapter begins with his second, longer stint as KU coach). In addition, some important statistics, records and lists can be found in the eighth chapter.

There's no need to read the Crimson and Blue Handbook from front to back (although that's perfectly acceptable). Pick it up and browse. Some entries will simply add to your knowledge of KU basketball. Others will undoubtedly prompt warm memories or maybe even righteous indignation. We're even looking for a chuckle here and there.

So sit back, hum a few bars of "The Crimson and the Blue," chant the "Rock Chalk Chant" to yourself, and enjoy.

Eric and Lauretta

TABLE OF CONTENTS

Chapter 1:
DR. JAMES A. NAISMITH (1898-1907)..........6

Chapter 2:
WILLIAM O. HAMILTON (1909-19)..........14

Chapter 3:
DR. F.C. "PHOG" ALLEN (1907-09, 1919-56)..........24

Chapter 4:
DICK HARP (1956-64)..........52

Chapter 5:
TED OWENS (1964-83)..........64

Chapter 6:
LARRY BROWN (1983-88)..........86

Chapter 7:
ROY WILLIAMS (1988-present)..........114

Chapter 8:
BY THE NUMBERS (Some KU Statistics)..........144

KU Quiz:
TRIVIA ANSWERS..........159

Dr. James A. Naismith

Years Coached at KU: 1898-1907
KU Record: 55-60, .478 winning percentage

Dr. James A. Naismith, working as a physical education instructor in Springfield, Mass., invented basketball in 1891. He brought the game to Lawrence seven years later, and life on Mount Oread has never been the same.

Naismith explained how he created the game in an article in the University Daily Kansan on Feb. 13, 1912:

"The game of basketball originated partly by the endeavor to create a form of athletic exercise along the line of football and partly by accident. ...

"It was while I was at the Springfield Training School in Massachusetts in 1891 that we discovered that the men who had played on the football team were not taking any interest in gymnasium exercise after the season had closed. They had been used to quick action, and pitting their wits against their opponents and the routine work with

James Naismith had asked for boxes as targets for his game, but only baskets were available.

dumbbells and Indian clubs was exceedingly irksome to them. The man who was the leader of the class became discouraged and gave it up, and I was invited to take his place. …

"At first we tried a form of 'dehorned' football, but that was too rough. Next followed soccer and then lacrosse, but none met the requirements of our small gymnasium. One day the question happened to strike me: What makes football rough? And the answer came – the tackling. …

"Why not eliminate the running, and that would eliminate the tackling. But you can't play a game and stand still all the while. Then I conceived the idea of letting all the men run except the man with the ball, and he would have to pass it before he could run. …

"I thought of the plan of turning the goal up horizontally so that the ball instead of being thrown in forcibly would have to describe an arc before it entered. I thought at first of placing it about two feet off the floor and then realized that all a goal keeper would have to do was to sit on it and it would be impossible for the opponents to score. I then thought of placing it up above the players' heads.

"I went to the janitor and asked for some sort of box. It just happened that he procured a couple of baskets (such as peaches are shipped in) about eighteen inches across the top and tapering down toward the bottom. We nailed these up on the gallery which happened to be just ten-feet high. The name 'basket ball' has clung to the game ever since, and the official height of the goals has remained just ten feet.

"The game was very successful in giving the men indoor excercise and training, and when vacation came in the summer, the men went to their various homes all over the United States and carried the game with them."

Naismith brought "basket ball" with him when he joined the faculty at the University of Kansas. But the Jayhawks took a while to master the game. Naismith's first team went 7-4, but he had only one other winning season and is the only KU coach with an overall losing record.

His contributions don't end with basketball. As a football player at Springfield College, Naismith had sliced a football lengthwise and had worn it on his head

KU QUIZ

1. Where was James Naismith born?

2. What is the oldest series between KU and a team now in the Big Eight Conference?

(Trivia answers start on page 159.)

Thirteen former Jayhawks are enshrined in the Naismith Memorial Basketball Hall of Fame in Springfield, Mass., more inductees than any other Division I school in the nation.

to protect his sore ears – the first football helmet.

Naismith, a minister and doctor, served as director of physical education at Kansas, retired in 1937 and died in 1939 at the age of 78. The national Basketball Hall of Fame, in Springfield, Mass., is named for him, and he was inducted to it in 1959.

1898-99: THE BEGINNING

The first game against outside competition came on Friday, Feb. 3, 1899, when KU traveled to Kansas City, Mo., to face the Kansas City YMCA.

The Jayhawks lost 16-5, but the student newspaper found plenty of ways to rationalize the loss:

K.U.'S FIRST GAME
Played At Kansas City Friday
Score 16-5 In Favor Of Kansas City

(*Kansas University Weekly, Feb. 4, 1899*)

"K.U. should not feel discouraged, but encouraged over the showing they made in their initial game.

"K.U. was handicapped by the fact that the baskets of the Y.M.C.A. club were fastened to the wall while those which the K.U. boys were accustomed to play with were about twelve feet from the wall. The game abounded in brilliant plays and from time to time plays brought forth tremendous applause from the audience.

"After one minute of play, owing to a foul, (Will) Sutton threw a goal. The playing from this time was exceedingly fast. The Y.M.C.A. after three minutes play threw a field goal. Sutton made one of the most sensational plays of the game one minute later. The ball was thrown to him, and he rolled it for three yards. He was viciously beset by two Y.M.C.A. men, and bending backward he threw the ball fully twelve yards and got a goal. The cheering at this good play was loud and long."

And that wasn't the only interesting tidbit about the first KU game. The Weekly also wrote about a player for the YMCA identified as Jesse James:

"The young man who has lately come into prominence by his alleged connection with recent train rob-

KU QUIZ

3. Who was the captain of KU's first team?

4. How was the first KU basketball team formed?

beries in Missouri played a rough and at times a very ungentlemanly game. He was cautioned and punished several times."

The player in question is thought to have been the son of the infamous Jesse James.

A six-game winning streak in the first season included a rematch victory against the Kansas City team. The Jayhawks finished the season 7-4, their last winning record until 1905-06.

"HEY, I INVENTED THIS GAME" During the 1900-01 season, KU, still coached by Naismith, walked off the court in an argument over the rules. The game was recorded as a 2-0 forfeit loss to the Ajax AC in Newton, Kan., on Dec. 22. The student paper carried an account:

"As stated, the game was a rough one, foul plays being numerous and many foot ball tactics being used. Calling fouls by the umpire only seemed to stimulate a desire for more rather than to lessen the offenses.

"The decision of the referee that caused the final dispute showed an inexcusable lack of knowledge of the rules, and our boys were indeed justified in leaving the field.

"Much of the rough playing might have been

The first Kansas team. Front row (left to right): Rusel Russell, Harold Hoyt and William Yahn. Middle row: Herbert Avery, Samuel Emley, William Sutton and William Hess. Back row: Frederick Owens, Willis Henderson, Walter Sutton and Dr. James Naismith. Not pictured: Eugene Owens and Eugene Queens.

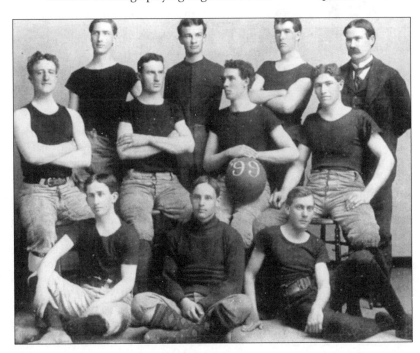

KU QUIZ

5. KU and visiting teams had interesting obstacles to deal with when they played in the basement of (old) Snow Hall. What were they?

avoided had the game not been played on a dancing floor. After the game, however, the Newton team, aided by friends, treated the boys to a dance, and the recent disputes were soon forgotten in the pleasures of the hour."

(Story in Kansas University Weekly, Jan. 12, 1901)

EARLY BASKET-BRAWL Chester A. Smith, a guard, was the captain of the 1901-02 team. In the January 1947 edition of the Graduate Magazine, he sought to shed some light on the early days of KU basketball:

"I think it was in 1901 or 1902 that the Athletic Association recognized basketball as a major sport and we were awarded basketball 'Ks'. [Editor's note: Lettermen are listed from as far back as KU's first season.]

"Noting the present comments on the recent tough schedules, reminds me of one trip the team (5 regulars and one substitute) made in 1902. We played a different team, in different cities, in six successive days. We looked and felt like the survivors of the Battle of the Bulge upon our

THE ROCK CHALK CHANT

R-o-c-k C-h-a-l-k,
J-a-y-h-a-w-k, K-U

R-o-c-k C-h-a-l-k,
J-a-y-h-a-w-k, K-U

Rock Chalk,
Jayhawk, KU

Rock Chalk,
Jayhawk, KU

Rock Chalk,
Jayhawk, KU

The famous Rock Chalk chant that resonates through a packed Allen Fieldhouse or echoes eerily around Memorial Stadium has a facinating history of its own.

According to accounts in the 1912 Kansan and the 1917 Jayhawker yearbook, the Rock Chalk chant originated in 1886. A science club at the university, started by a group of instructors that included chemistry professor E.H.S. Bailey, wanted to come up with a yell for their club.

The club members took monthly marches over the hills around Lawrence, collecting specimens for the zoology and geology classes. Bailey developed the chant for those monthly treks.

"We used it with such success on our picnics and excursions that it was soon taken up by the student return to K.U.

"The rules in these days were not quite so rigid on what constituted a foul; hence the game was plenty rough. Only 'strangle holds,' eye-gouging and a few other such minor practices were barred and were cause for a foul whistle.

"Dear old Dr. Naismith was our coach but did not accompany the team on trips. The Athletic Association furnished us a basketball. Individual players furnished their own uniforms, and a student manager made the schedules and financed the trips by guarantees from the opponents."

Chester A. Smith, e '04
Kansas City, Mo.

Early accounts spelled Allen's nickname Fog, but it was later changed to Phog.

PHOG ALERT At the beginning of the 1905-06 season, the big news surrounded a certain freshman player: Forrest C. Allen. Expectations were high, but no one could have known the impact he would have on Kansas basketball.

"Forrest Allen made his first appearance at basketball in the gymnasium Thursday evening. The ceiling was too low for him to show how well body at large and made the regular yell of the University," Bailey wrote in the 1917 Jayhawker, which was dedicated to the chant. "And so the yell that sounds o'er land and sea was introduced to K.U."

Bailey also wrote that the early yell was "Rah, Rah, Jay Hawk, KU," being repeated three times. An English professor reportedly suggested "Rock Chalk" because it rhymed with Jayhawk and "was also symbolic of the chalky limestone formations found on Mount Oread."

The Kansan's history of the chant, published on March 4, 1912, says the chant's form of two drawn-out chanted lines followed by three quick lines came about in 1905.

Ever since the yell's inception, it has also been used by Kansans in the military, including during the Spanish-American War and the Boxer Rebellion in China.

A report from the National Tribune in 1918 told of Kansans using the yell in World War I to convince "the Kaiser that an imported cyclone has been let loose. ... It's classed as a college yell, but Rock Chalk is really more than that."

Much more. Fans across the country are familiar with the chant, and when Kansas advanced to the Final Four in Indianapolis in 1991, the KU contingent's yell silenced the crowd before the championship game against Duke. As "Rock Chalk, Jayhawk" echoed through the Hoosier Dome, even the rowdy Blue Devil fans could be seen sitting in awe.

KU QUIZ

6. Robinson Gymnasium was built for the 1907-08 season. How much did it cost to build?

7. How many fans did it seat?

8. Whom was it named after?

he could throw long goals, but he gave the men some good ideas of how to get into the game. Allen will be able to play in the games in this year's schedule and will make a strong addition to the team. He is one of the world's champions and is said to be the best goal thrower in the world."

(Story in the Kansan, Oct. 18, 1905)

Allen quickly lived up to the hype. On Feb. 12, 1906, he played in his first first full game, a 37-17 win at Nebraska. The Kansan reported, "Fog Allen did star work at forward, making 23 out of the 37 points."

Despite playing only three home games, KU finished the season 12-7, Naismith's only other winning mark other than his first season.

Phog Allen resigned as captain of the 1906-07 team and left the university to become head basketball coach at Baker University in Baldwin City, Kan. The idea seemed preposterous to Naismith, who once told Allen, "You can't coach the game of basketball; you just play it."

FARMERS AND SOLDIERS AND TEACHERS, OH MY! KU's
schedule in 1906-07 included "the Farmers of Manhattan, the Soldiers of Fort Riley, the Teachers of Emporia, the Methodists of Baldwin, and the Athletics of Newton."

The Jayhawks lost to Allen's Baker team 39-24.

1907-08: THE FIRST CONFERENCE CHAMPIONSHIP

The Missouri Valley Conference was officially organized in 1907-08. The champions of the first 10 seasons:
1. Kansas
2. Kansas
3. Kansas
4. Kansas
5. Kansas/Nebraska
6. Nebraska
7. Kansas/Nebraska
8. Kansas
9. Nebraska
10. Kansas State

Phog Allen returned to KU as head coach for the 1907-08 and 1908-09 seasons before leaving the university for 10 seasons.

The Jayhawks went 6-0 in Missouri Valley Conference play in 1907-08, claiming their first league championship. KU was playing in its new home, Robinson Gymnasium, and the 1908 Jayhawker yearbook reported that the championship season saw student enthusiasm for basketball reach new levels.

"The crowds ranged everywhere from two hundred up to a thousand, while for enthusiasm even the most exciting Foot-ball contests could hardly have equaled the rooting and yelling at the spectacular Basket-ball contests this winter."

The first championship team was led by George McCune, who was from Leavenworth, Kan. The yearbook reported that he "played a steady, consistent game at forward all season, netting many and many a point for

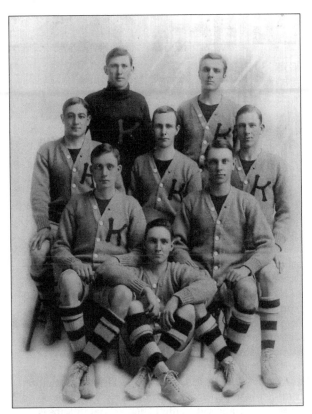

Phog Allen, back left, coached the 1907-08 KU team to the first Missouri Valley Conference championship. The conference was created after a Jan. 12, 1907, meeting in Kansas City, Mo.

his squad with his accurate goal shooting."

Earl "Woodie" Woodward also played an important role from his guard position and was voted captain for the following season. The yearbook listed the other key players as "Billy" Miller, Milton Miller and Ralph Bergen.

9. Who was the captain of KU's first Missouri Valley Conference championship team?

William O. Hamilton

Years Coached at KU: 1909-1919
KU Record:125-59, .679 winning percentage

Perhaps unfairly, William O. Hamilton seems to be best known for "filling in" the gap for the 10 seasons between Phog Allen's two stints as head coach of the Jayhawks. In fact, Hamilton's record, especially through his first six seasons, was impressive. Hamilton's Jayhawks won the Missouri Valley Conference in his first three seasons. In his first six seasons, the Jayhawks collected four outright titles, one co-championship and one second-place finish.

Hamilton's teams produced the Valley scoring champion five times, with the honor going three times to Ralph "Lefty" Sproull, an All-American in the 1914-15 season. Hamilton also coached two other All-Americans, Tommy Johnson and Arthur C. "Dutch" Lonborg.

Hamilton came to KU in 1909 and served as the university's athletic director from 1911 to 1919. Before coming to Lawrence, Hamilton had been director of physical education at Central High School in Kansas City, Mo., and at William Jewell College in Liberty, Mo.

After resigning in 1919, Hamilton concentrated on his automobile dealership and stayed in Lawrence until his death on Dec. 30, 1951.

10. What other sport did William Hamilton coach?

1909-10: HAMILTON'S ERA BEGINS

During Hamilton's first season, the Jayhawks won the school's third Missouri Valley basketball championship.

Led by team captain Tommy Johnson, KU lost only once. And that was in dispute. "Technically the game belonged to Kansas," the 1910 yearbook declared.

The Jayhawks lost to Washington University 16-15 on Feb. 20, 1910, in St. Louis. The Kansan blamed the loss on poor officiating:

> "In the second half the Kansans were busy and up to the last three minutes of plays held a two point lead. The referee who had up to this time been entirely unconscious of fouls, suddenly had a reversal of form and called four in succession on

the Kansas men. …

"Johnson threw a basket, and while the ball was in the air, the final whistle blew. The referee, with entire disregard for the rules which allows such goals to count, threw out the resulting two points, and Kansas lost."

GOOD EYE, COACH On more than one occasion, Hamilton was noted for his sharp eye in checking dimensions.

"When the Jayhawkers stepped into the limelight at the Kansas City Athletic Club Friday evening, the eagle eye of Coach Hamilton discovered that there was something wrong with the measurements of the basket-ball court. A tape line was called for, and it was found that the line from which free throws are made was back two feet too far. After the mistake had been rectified and some opinions expressed, the game began."

(Story in the Kansan, Feb. 19, 1910)

EARLY BORDER WARS From the very beginning, games between Kansas and Missouri seemed to take on a spe-

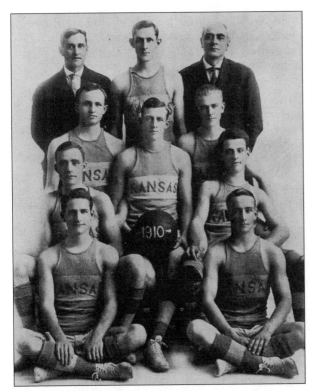

The 1909-10 Jayhawks. Front row (from left to right:): Donald Martindell, Edward Van der Vries.
Second row: Earl Woodward, Verne Long.
Third row: Harold Larson, Thomas Johnson, Verni Smith.
Fourth row: William Hamilton, Robert Heizer and W.C. Lansdon.

cial feel – usually rough, according to accounts such as this one in the Kansan on Feb. 12, 1910, regarding a Jayhawk victory in Lawrence:

TIGER'S TAIL WAS TWISTED
Hamilton's Five Tied 29 Knots In It
The Game Last Night Was A Cross Between Football And Wrestling - To Clash Again Tonight

"It has been officially announced that spring football practice has started at Missouri University, and verily we believe it. What is more, all the men who played in the 'near' basket-ball game last night must be out for the team.

"Kansas got away with the game by a 29 to 15 tally and was mighty lucky to have as wide a margin as that, for it is not conducive to fast basket-ball to spend half of the time getting off the floor and the other half escaping the embraces of your opponents."

INVENTION GONE BAD Dr. James Naismith cringed at some of the roughly played games of this era. The Kansan reported his concern in its Feb. 15, 1910, edition after a game with Missouri.

"'Oh, gracious! They are murdering my game!' quoth Dr. Jas. Naismith, in sorrowful tones, as Tiger and Jayhawk roughed it back and forth over the basket ball court Saturday night: and truly, the University authority on the 'The Principles of Sports and Games' had reason to be sad. The game, however, was a satisfactory affair. It was only another step in the terrible revenge that is due to fall on the head of old Missou. The score was 27 to 14, with (Tommy) Johnson's bunch on the long end."

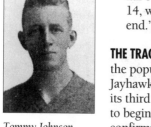

Tommy Johnson was KU's first All-American.

THE TRAGIC CASE OF TOMMY JOHNSON Tommy Johnson, the popular KU forward who in 1909 became the Jayhawks' first All-American in any sport, had led KU to its third Valley title in 1909-10. But as the team prepared to begin games in 1911, the Jan. 24 Kansan ran a story confirming that Johnson would not play for the team that year. It reported that Johnson had voluntarily withdrawn from athletics after reports surfaced that he had

become academically ineligible.

In fact, Johnson had become quite ill with tuberculosis. Johnson had become involved in athletics mainly to improve his physical condition. After spending much of the spring and summer of 1911 in Missouri trying to regain his health, Johnson was hospitalized back in Kansas and died on Nov. 24, 1911, at the age of 24. He had captained the 1909 and 1910 basketball teams and the 1910 football team and had run the high hurdles and pole-vaulted for the track team. He earned 11 letters at KU and also was involved in school plays.

The loss of Johnson was a blow to Jayhawk fans. The Kansan later reprinted a poem written by a W.N. Randolph that had run in the Kansas City Star. In part, it read:

"Now let the waving pennons droop
And hush the battle trumpets' roar.
As friend and foe the head bow low,
For Tommy Johnson is no more."

Kansas played in Robinson Gymnasium for 20 years, winning 79.6 percent of its games. The gym had a capacity of 3,000 people.

1910-11: A VALLEY FOUR-PEAT

KU finished 12-6 overall and 9-3 in the Valley, and that was good enough for another league crown. But all three conference losses were against Nebraska, a fact not taken lightly in an article in the Feb. 28, 1911, Kansan:

JAYHAWKS ARE VALLEY CHAMPIONS
Heizer's Squad Lost But Three Conference Games
Despite Poor Record on the Recent Trip,
Kansas Won Most Games - Individual Scores

"This is the fourth time premier honors of the Valley have been won by the Jayhawkers, but this time a stigma is cast upon the title by reason of the fact that the Cornhuskers defeated the champions three times out of the four games played. However, the basketball championship is determined by the number of games won and lost by members of the Conference and since Kansas has only three defeats in the Missouri Valley to her credit, a record which is better than that of any other member of the Conference, the right of Kansas to

THE JAYHAWK OVER THE YEARS

The Jayhawk is a mythical bird that has been associated with the University of Kansas since the Rock Chalk chant came into being in 1886. The term goes back as far as 1849 and was first used by pioneers heading west. About 1858, the term was used in Kansas to refer to "robbing, looting and general lawlessness," according to the KU media guide, but in the Civil War, it came to be associated with those fighting to keep Kansas a free state.

The Jayhawk has evolved since the first artist's rendition in 1912.

1912: Drawn by Henry Maloy, a KU student from Eureka, Kan.

1920: The artist of this somber Jayhawk is unknown.

first place cannot be disputed."

Three KU players were named to the first Valley All-Conference team for the 1910-1911 season: Verne Long, Bob Heizer and Don Dousman. Long was also the league scoring champion, averaging 12.3 points a game.

LIKE MIKE Michael Jordan is generally credited with inspiring the current style of long basketball shorts. But the Jayhawks were well ahead of the game's fashion trends. The Kansan ran this story on Jan. 19, 1911:

Bob Heizer played center for KU from 1909 to 1911 and was a Jayhawk captain.

> "Truly the chorus girl with the abbreviated costume and Coach Hamilton's basket-ball tossers have a common bond of sympathy. If a bill passes, the garments worn by the pony ballet during its sojourn in Kansas must reach below the patella.
>
> "Dr. James Naismith has decided that the idea is a good one and has issued an edict that all goal shooters representing the University must take precautions before entering a game to see that their patellas are properly excluded from the curious gaze of student onlookers."

GETTING ALL THE FREEBIES A rule allowing one man to shoot every free throw paid off for Verne "Shorty" Long

1923: Two KU students, George Hollingbery and Jimmy O'Bryon, drew this version.

1941: This Jayhawk, close to the modern rendition, was drawn by Gene Williams.

1929: The "Fighting Jayhawk" was drawn by KU student Forrest O. Calvin.

1946: The modern, smiling Jayhawk was drawn by Harold D. Sandy and is still in use.

Verne Long played forward for the Jayhawks from 1909 to 1911.

in 1910-1911. He made 137 of the 138 successful free throws for the Jayhawks that year. Donald Dousman was the only other player to sink one from the free-throw line.

1911-12: WHO'S THE CHAMP?

The Jayhawks' rivalry with Nebraska seemed to heat up with each passing season, and in the Jan. 22, 1912, edition of The University Daily Kansan, two losses to the Cornhuskers were reported under a headline that was sizeable for the times:

CATCH AS CATCH CAN BOUTS WERE STAGED
Alleged Basket Ball Games
Were High Class Wrestling Tournaments
NEBRASKA WON BOTH FALLS
The Contestants Were Adept With
The Toe Hold, Strangle Hold,
And the Other Holds

KU lost those games to Nebraska 30-26 and 30-27. But at least the games' entertainment value was noted: "All in all the games were fine ones for the spectators. There was plenty to laugh about, and several things to howl about. What more is wanted for a basket-ball game?"

The drama with Nebraska that season was just beginning to unfold. KU won the Valley's southern division while Nebraska took the northern division. The teams were scheduled to meet to determine the conference title.

After weeks and weeks of haggling about officials, financial guarantees and playing sites, the schools were unable to agree on a suitable format for a championship series, and the teams were eventually named co-champs.

KU's Loren "Red" Brown was the conference scoring champion for the 1911-1912 season, averaging 13.3 points a game.

TOUGH TALK Hamilton vowed he would not play the Cornhuskers during the 1912-13 season unless games were needed to decide the conference championship. But

KU QUIZ

11. In the 1912-1913 season, KU trounced Washington (Mo.) 68-8 in Lawrence. One Jayhawk scored 40 points in the game. Who was he?

they were needed, and KU lost two of three in a title series, failing to secure a share of the title for the first time since joining the Missouri Valley Conference for the 1907-08 season.

BUT THEY SURE LOOKED SPIFFY The Kansan carried a description of KU's new uniforms on Jan. 19, 1913:

> "The new Varsity suits have a V-neck jersey with a blue body and carry a red stripe around the chest and neck. The pants are of khaki with blue stripes down the sides and around the bottom. The shoes are of white elk skin with heavy red rubber soles. The stockings are of red and blue. Altogether this is a very good looking as well as novel suit and probably is unmatched in the Missouri Valley."

WHO'S THAT IN THE CRIMSON AND BLUE? On Feb. 19, 1914, KU met Phog Allen's Warrensburg team (now Central Missouri State University), which came to play in Lawrence wearing red and blue uniforms similar to those of the Jayhawks. According to the Kansan, it was not until Hamilton "called his team from the floor and decorated them with grey jerseys" that the game could be played. KU won 49-22.

EARLY ANTLERS? From early on, the fans at Missouri made life on the road tough for the Jayhawks.

During the 1913-14 season, an account in the student paper reported that the "Missouri rooters" were called for a foul. And in the 1919-1920 season, the Kansan reported that the Missouri fans "yelled with delight" when Dutch Lonborg twisted his knee.

WE'RE GOING TO OVERTIME With the start of the 1914-15 season, a new rule allowed for a five-minute overtime period if the game was tied at the end of regulation. Before this, the team that scored the first three points after a tie was declared the winner. KU made use of the new rule, beating Iowa State in overtime during the second game of the season, 27-23.

1914-15: HAMILTON'S LAST TITLE

The Jayhawks were 16-1 and compiled a 13-1 conference record in 1914-15, winning what would be their last Valley championship until 1922 and their last under Hamilton.

Led by All-Conference players Ralph "Lefty" Sproull, Ephraim Sorensen, Arthur Weaver and Ray "Stuffy"

12. The crowd at the KU-K-State game on Feb. 11, 1915, included an unusual spectator. Who was this Tiger, and why was he there?

13. In the 1915-16 season, KU lost its first non-conference game during William Hamilton's tenure. Who was the opponent?

14. Ralph "Lefty" Sproull was back on the KU scene for the 1915-16 season. In what capacity?

The 1913-14 KU team. Front row (from left to right:): Edward Van der Vries, Charles Greenlees, Ray Dunmire and Ray Folks. Second row: William Weidlein, William Hamilton, Ralph Sproull and Homer Hargiss. Third row: Lawrence Cole, Arthur Weaver and Lester Smith.

Ralph "Lefty" Sproull was the league scoring champion in 1914-15, averaging 17.8 points a game. He also had led the Valley in scoring the previous two seasons, averaging 14.1 points in 1912-13 and 15.5 in 1913-1914. He was named All-American in 1915, the second Jayhawk to be so honored.

Dunmire, KU's only loss was to what is now Kansas State.

Game accounts blamed the 21-18 loss on the fact that two Jayhawk starters had the mumps. Sproull also was reported as sick, but he played.

MUMPS AND AGGIES TOO MUCH FOR KU

(Headline of the University Daily Kansan, Feb. 11, 1915)

TOUGH TIMES FOR THE JAYHAWKS The last four years of Hamilton's tenure grew increasingly grim as KU twice finished fourth in the conference, once third, and, finally, fifth in 1918-19.

But with World War I in full swing, basketball was not foremost on most minds.

The 1915-16 season was Hamilton's first losing season, with KU finishing 6-12 overall and 5-11 in the Valley. The bright spot came when KU ruined Missouri's perfect record by beating the Tigers 31-19 in the final game of the season.

In 1916-17, Hamilton began naming his starting players only minutes before each game. He had found that when he named his starters in advance, several of the other players failed to show up for the game. The Jayhawks began the year 7-0 but collapsed, collecting a second-straight fourth-place finish.

KU finished third in 1917-18. Missouri's perfect MVC season once again was spoiled by KU when Hamilton altered his lineup on Feb. 21 and beat the Tigers.

1918-19: HAMILTON CALLS IT QUITS

The Jayhawks wound up 7-9 overall and 5-9 in the Valley – good enough, or bad enough, for a fifth-place finish.

It would be their lowest conference finish until the 1947-1948 season.

Trouble hit before the season even started. Howard "Scrubby" Laslett had been elected as captain for the 1918-19 team and would have been only the second Jayhawk to serve as both football captain and basketball captain in the same year. But by the time the season started, Laslett was in France with a tank battalion and senior center Kelsey Matthews was chosen as captain in his place.

Three coaches in the athletic department and Naismith, the director of physical education, were on leave for service in the war. Hamilton had taken over Naismith's duties, a position he resigned on Feb. 25, 1919, with perhaps a glimpse of what was to come: "The department of athletics has been working under serious handicap since the declaration of war," he said. "An elephant's job was thrown upon my shoulders."

Standouts John Bunn and Arthur Lonborg began their KU careers that season but were not enough to pull the Jayhawks from the lower division of the conference.

On June 10, 1919, Hamilton officially resigned from coaching, turning his attention to his car dealership.

KU QUIZ

15. On Feb. 28, 1916, Missouri beat KU 41-10. What was significant about this Jayhawk loss?

16. Who selected the 1917-1918 All-Valley team?

17. On the 1917-18 KU team, there were two players nick-named "Dutch." Of course, there was Arthur Lonborg. But who else answered to this name?

DR. FORREST C. "PHOG" ALLEN

Years Coached at KU: 1907-1909, 1919-1956
KU Record: 590-219, .729 winning percentage

Phog Allen applied for the athletic director vacancy at K-State in 1915 while he was coaching at Warrensburg (Mo.) Teachers College. The job was instead given to Z.G. Clevenger, who later became athletic director at Missouri. Allen said it "was the first time I didn't get a job I applied for. ... Since then, whenever we play K-State, I try to prove to them that I might have been a success."

It's been almost 40 years since he coached his last game at KU, but the image of "Phog" Allen still looms large at the University of Kansas and at the fieldhouse that bears his name.

His legacy lives in the banners that decorate the fieldhouse ceiling. They mark the 24 conference championships won during his reign; his national championship team of 1952 that went on to Olympic glory; his teams of 1922 and 1923 that were later named national champions; and his national finalists of 1940 and 1953.

And high in the rafters hangs another banner: "Beware of the Phog." The message serves not so much as a warning but as a reminder of KU's rich tradition.

Allen was born Nov. 18, 1885, in Jamesport, Mo. He was the fourth of six sons in an athletic family. He first came to KU in 1905, and played basketball for the Jayhawks under "The Father of Basketball," Dr. James Naismith. He earned three letters between 1905 and 1907.

"The Father of Basketball Coaching," as he was later

called by Naismith, began his fabled coaching career in 1907, splitting time between three teams – KU, Baker University and Haskell Institute – until 1909.

After a short time away from the game, Allen headed to Warrensburg Teachers College (now Central Missouri State) in 1912 to become the coach of their athletic teams. His record was 102-7 during his seven years coaching the basketball team, and he won seven conference championships.

He returned to Kansas in 1919 as athletic director. Later that year, he took over as head basketball coach. And there he stayed until age 70, when he was forced to retire after the 1956 season.

Allen, highly outspoken on most subjects involving basketball and on a few other topics, as well, was a longtime critic of the Amateur Athletic Union, eastern basketball's alleged ties to gambling and of scandals of any sort involving the game.

He and his wife, Bessie, had six children. Two of his sons, Milton and Bob, lettered under their father while playing at KU.

Phog Allen, who was a trained osteopath, had a

KU QUIZ

18. How did Phog Allen get his nickname?

19. Phog Allen went by another name to those who were closest to him. What was it?

PHOG'S ACCOMPLISHMENTS

While at KU, Phog Allen:

■ Became the winningest coach in Kansas basketball history, and his career victory total of 746 has been surpassed only by two of his former players – Adolph Rupp of Kentucky and Dean Smith of North Carolina.

■ Helped found the National Basketball Coaches Association, which he headed from 1927 through 1929.

■ Was instrumental in starting the NCAA Tournament in 1939.

■ Was a driving force in the push to introduce basketball as an Olympic sport in the 1936 Games.

■ Served as an assistant coach on the 1952 gold-medal Olympic basketball team.

■ Was named national Coach of the Year in 1950.

■ Was a member of the basketball rules committee for 13 years and once served as its vice president.

■ Helped establish the Kansas Relays in 1923.

■ Coached football in 1920, going 5-2-1; and coached baseball two seasons, 1941 and '42, going 6-17.

■ Was instrumental in the drive to build Memorial Stadium.

■ Was awarded the University of Kansas and Alumni Association Distinguished Service Citation in 1966. It is the highest honor the university bestows.

■ Authored three books about basketball: "Basketball Bible" in 1924, "Better Basketball" in 1936, and "Phog Allen's Sports Stories" in 1947.

In 1904, Phog Allen and his five brothers formed their own basketball team. Homer was the oldest at 28 and served as the substitute, while Richard, 13, was the youngest starter. The Allens played for four seasons against teams in Missouri and Kansas and lost only one game, 40-39 against Baker. The game had been scheduled by Phog Allen, the coach at Baker who played for the Allens that day.

John Bunn earned 10 letters playing three sports at KU.

Arthur Lonborg later served as KU's athletic director.

practice in Lawrence for 10 years after his retirement from coaching. He stayed in Lawrence until his death on Sept. 16, 1974, at the age of 88.

Allen, who was elected to the Naismith Memorial Basketball Hall of Fame in 1959, is remembered as a master motivator and molder of men.

1919-20: THE PHOG RETURNS

After William Hamilton resigned, Karl Schlademan, head track coach at KU, began the 1919-1920 season as the Jayhawks' basketball coach. But he didn't last long. Kansas beat Emporia State 37-22 in the season opener, and Schlademan promptly resigned to concentrate on his track duties. Allen stepped in, leading the Jayhawks to an 11-7 record and a third-place finish in the Valley. It was the first time in his coaching career that his basketball team had not won a league title.

But it wasn't the last.

John Bunn and All-American Arthur "Dutch" Lonborg had been around to help the 1919-1920 team. But by the 1920-21 season, they had graduated. Without their leadership, KU slipped further, finishing 10-8 for fourth place in the Valley.

NOT THROUGH AT KU Although finished playing, Bunn and Lonborg were far from finished with the game of basketball or the University of Kansas.

Bunn was the first KU athlete to earn 10 letters, playing football, basketball and baseball. From 1924 to 1927, he coached freshman football, basketball and baseball. He went on to coach basketball for 42 years at Stanford University, Springfield (Mass.) College and Northern Colorado. He was instrumental in getting the Naismith Hall of Fame named after the former KU coach, and he was elected to the hall in 1964.

Lonborg, also a three-sport letterman at KU, was named All-Valley in 1919 and 1920 and All-American in 1919. He graduated from the KU law school and coached basketball at McPherson (Kan.) College and Washburn University in Topeka, Kan. He then coached at Northwestern for 23 years. He helped get the NCAA Tournament started in 1939 and returned to KU in 1950, where he served as athletic director for 14 years. He was elected to the Naismith Hall of Fame in 1972.

CHEAP SEATS Single admission to a KU game in 1921 was 75 cents. The die-hard fan could purchase a season ticket for 10 conference games for $5.

HOLIDAY TUNEUP During the Christmas holidays of the 1921-22 season, Allen took his team to Minneapolis, Minn., where the Jayhawks practiced for a week against the Minnesota Gophers. They played a game at the end of the week, and KU won 32-11. The Gophers went on to finish third in the Big Ten, and Allen credited the work in Minnesota as helping his team in the more physical games later that season.

1921-22: BACK ON TOP

KU went 16-2 overall and 15-1 in the Valley, tying Missouri for the conference title. George Rody and Paul Endacott led the Jayhawks on a team that later was declared national champion by the Helms Foundation of Los Angeles. Rody was the conference scoring leader, averaging 15.2 points per game, and Endacott was named All-American.

1922-23: "EVER-VICTORIOUS"

The Jayhawks became the first team to complete an undefeated season in the Valley. Not exactly "ever-victorious" as they were dubbed, the Jayhawks lost one non-conference game 27-23 to the Kansas City Athletic Club. The Jayhawks, 17-1 overall and 16-0 in the Valley,

The 1921-22 Kansas team. Front row (from left to right): George Glaskin, Paul Endacott, George Staplin and Floyd Dillenbeck. Second row: Edmund Speck, Dee Mifflin, John Wulf, George Rody, Johnson, Herbert Olson and Charlie T. Black. Back row: A.E. Woestemeyer, John Lonborg, Phog Allen, Adolph Rupp, Andrew McDonald and Waldo Bowman.

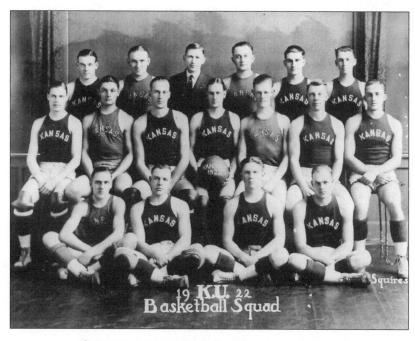

were later designated the 1923 national champions by the Helms Foundation. Endacott and Charlie Black were All-Americans on the team, and John Wulf joined them on the all-conference team. Tusten Ackerman, who also played on the 1923 squad, went on to All-American honors in 1924 and 1925.

Three-thousand fans packed Robinson Gymnasium on Feb. 28, 1923, to watch KU clinch the title and an unbeaten record with a 23-20 victory against Missouri.

The Kansan gave this account of the finish:

MISSOURIANS CRUMBLE BEFORE ATTACK OF ALLEN COURT SQUAD;
Kansans Are Valley Champs

(Headline of The University Daily Kansan, March 1, 1923)

Phog's undefeated teams (in conference play):
1922-23: 16-0
1935-36: 10-0
1942-43: 10-0
1945-46: 10-0

"The play was on again, and breathlessly the crowd followed every move of the ball. Bang! The crack of the pistol split the air. For a moment everyone sat silent, unable to realize that it was all over – that Kansas had defeated Missouri again, and that K.U. had an all-victorious basketball team – the first in the history of the Valley.

Suddenly they realized the great climax, and rising to their feet roared forth the "Crimson and the Blue," with the hearts full of joy and minds teeming with memory of a great basketball battle and victory."

Paul Endacott was inducted to the Naismith Hall of Fame in 1971.

THE AMAZING "ENDY" Paul Endacott was captain of the 1923 team and was later named Player of the Year by the Helms Foundation. Allen called him "the greatest player I have ever coached," and was fond of telling about Endacott's heroics during KU's game at Missouri on Jan. 16, 1923, which the Jayhawks won 21-19. Endacott had grabbed 16 straight jump balls in the closing minutes to preserve the win. He later collapsed in the locker room from exhaustion.

But Allen always said he was most proud of his players' accomplishments later in life and often mentioned Endacott, who became president of Phillips Petroleum Company.

PHOG'S FAVORITE

"For its size and talent, the 1923 team did more than any other team I ever had. Paul Endacott was only about 6 feet tall, but he was a basketball player deluxe. We old-timers naturally think the old-time teams were better. I think we played more clever basketball. … In the pro game now, it's just shoot, score and run, shoot, score and run, over and over."

(Phog Allen in the Kansas City
Star Magazine, March 26, 1972)

SNOB HILL VS. SILO TECH Even early on, stereotypes about K-State's agricultural background were perpetuated by students, especially through the KU school newspaper:

KANSAS COURTSTERS BEAT AGGIE QUINTET IN BITTER CONTEST
Agriculturalists Close Gap in Score by Brilliant Rally but are Headed by Allenites

(The University Daily Kansan, Feb.21, 1923)

"Bedlam broke loose again as the Kansans took their allotted two minutes out for a tete-a-tete. A cow over in the experiment station on the campus swallowed her cud in the excitement. Aggie rooters

The 1922-23 Kansas team (from left to right): Phog Allen, Paul Endacott, Charlie T. Black, A.E. Woestemeyer, Waldo Bowman, Andrew McDonald, Adolph Rupp, Verne Wilkin, Bob Moseby, Tusten Ackerman, Byron Frederick and John Wulf.

Phog Allen considered his 1923 team, shown at a reunion in 1968, his greatest based on the players' accomplishments after graduating from KU.
Front row (from left to right): A.E. Woestemeyer, Waldo Bowman, Paul Endacott and Andrew McDonald.
Second row: John Wulf, Phog Allen and Charlie T. Black.
Back row: Adolph Rupp, Tusten Ackerman and Verne Wilkin.

threw eight-dollar derbies into the air and hugged their neighbors. The stands rocked."

"THE BARON OF BASKETBALL" Adolph Rupp, who was from Halstead, Kan., was a reserve on KU's 1922 and 1923 championship teams, but his basketball accomplishments were far from over. He went on to coach at Kentucky for 41 years, and his 880-190 record surpassed Allen's as the winningest college coaching record. He led his Kentucky teams to 27 Southeastern Conference championships and four national titles. He was elected to the Naismith Hall of Fame in 1959.

MEMORIAL STADIUM A second-half rally by the Allen-coached Kansas football team against Nebraska in 1920 sparked the drive to build a new football stadium. Trailing 20-0 at halftime, KU scored three second-half touchdowns for a 20-20 tie at old McCook Field.

Allen took great pride in his involvement in the building of Memorial Stadium. He said, "Of course it is fine to win in basketball, as it is in all other sports," but went on to add that his part in completing the stadium was "the most delightful and gratifying thing that has come to me in athletics."

ROUGH START IN A NEW HOME The first game in KU's Hoch Auditorium was Jan. 6, 1928, a 29-26 victory against Washington University of St. Louis. Hoch would see many conference championships won by KU, but not that first season. The Jayhawks finished 9-9, fourth in the Valley. Those nine defeats, all in conference play, gave KU more conference losses than in its previous six seasons combined.

Kentucky coach Adolph Rupp was a reserve on KU's 1922 and 1923 championship teams. He is the winningest college coach of all time.

ROUGHER START IN A NEW CONFERENCE The 1928-29 season was even worse as the Jayhawks went 3-15 overall and 2-8 and finished fifth in their first season in the Big Six Conference, which later became the Big Eight.

QUICK RECOVERY The Jayhawks, with All-American Forrest "Frosty" Cox, rebounded for a second-place Big Six finish in 1929-30 before winning four straight conference titles. In that span, KU was led by Cox, Tom Bishop and All-Americans Ted O'Leary and Bill "Skinny" Johnson, who was elected to the Naismith Hall of Fame in 1976 as the dominant center of his time.

A GOOD PACE In 1931-32, Allen won his 10th conference title in 15 years of coaching at KU. The Jayhawks won or shared seven of the eight league titles from 1931 to 1938 and finished second in 1935.

The 1928 team runs drills in Robinson Gymnasium.

"Kansas teams step on the court with a feeling that they have a tradition to uphold, and nine times out of ten they uphold it," KU All-American Ted O'Leary wrote in 1932.

BOOING THE BOO Allen loved crowd support, as long it wasn't negative toward either team. In 1933, he said he would work "against blatant rowdyism, expressed in the form of booing, hissing, and the well-known 'Bronx cheer.'...

"I think that booing and rowdyism are getting so bad that unless definite steps are taken to curtail them, they will kill the game."

The 1935-36 Kansas team, pictured below, won 21 straight games. When Utah State beat the Jayhawks on March 26, 1936, in the Olympic playoffs, it ended a 23-game winning streak that is still the longest in KU history.

THE GAME ACCORDING TO PHOG Allen, who served as chairman of the research committee of the National Basketball Rules Committee, pushed for several rule changes throughout his career – especially raising the goals to 12 feet, which he felt would de-emphasize post play.

"If we raised the goals" he said in 1940, "these mezzanine-peeping goons wouldn't be able to score like little children pushing pennies into gum machines. They would have to throw the ball like anyone else. They would have to make the team on real skill, not merely on height."

KU opened the 1934-35 season with two games against Kansas State played with 12-foot baskets. Each basket on the higher goals counted for three points. The first game was played at Hoch Auditorium on Dec. 14, 1934, and Kansas lost 39-35. But the Jayhawks won the second "experimental game," which was played in Manhattan on Dec. 18, 1934, by a score of 40-26.

During the experiment, Ray Ebling became the first Jayhawk to hit a 3-pointer.

1935-36: SHOOTING FOR BERLIN

The Jayhawks, led by All-Big Six players Ray Ebling, Francis Kappelman and Fred Pralle, won 21 straight games in the 1935-36 season. Ebling, a native of Lindsborg, Kan., was named All-American in 1936, and Pralle was named All-American the following two years.

Ebling, one of two "Death Rays" on the 1935-36 team (the other was Ray Noble), was the first player to lead the Big Six in scoring for three straight seasons. He averaged 14.1 points a game in 1935-36 as KU advanced to the Olympic playoffs. The Jayhawks beat Washburn and Oklahoma State to win the district playoffs and advanced to meet Utah State for a three-game series. KU won the first game 39-37 in overtime but lost the last two games, ending its Olympic bid. The first loss to Utah State ended a 23-game KU winning streak, still the longest in Jayhawk history.

Allen, however, had already been slated to head the 1936 basketball team in Berlin. It was an honor he forfeited, however, as he resigned in one of his many disputes with the AAU.

DEANER Dean Nesmith was a three-year letterman as a tackle on KU's football team and went on to play one year of professional football before earning his degree in 1937. He joined the KU athletic staff as trainer a year later, beginning a 46-year tenure with KU athletic teams. He retired in 1983.

All of KU's biggest stars in every sport during that era worked with the "Deaner" at some point: Wilt Chamberlain, Clyde Lovellette, Gayle Sayers, Al Oerter, Jim Ryun, John Hadl, Jo Jo White and Nolan Cromwell. He was the trainer for the 1960 U.S. Olympic basketball team and toured Yugoslavia with the Big Eight All-Star basketball team in 1974. He died Sept. 25, 1985, at the age of 71.

At a ceremony in his honor during halftime of a 1984

Eight of KU's longest winning streaks occurred during the Allen era, including the longest: 23 games over the 1934-35 and 1935-36 seasons. Other streaks during Allen's tenure:

22 games: 1907-08 to 1908-09

18 games: 1925-26 to 1926-27

16 games: 1950-51 to 1951-52

15 games: 1951-52

13 games: 1924-25

12 games: 1933-34

12 games: 1942-43

Dean Nesmith lettered from 1933 to 1935 as a tackle on the KU football team. He was a trainer at KU for 46 years.

basketball game, Nesmith told the crowd: "I'm the luckiest man in the world because through all these years, there was never a day I didn't look forward to going to work. It was going to a job I thoroughly loved and enjoyed. How can you be luckier than that?"

FALSE PROPHECY Allen drew some fire in 1940 with his statement that college football was dying and would be around for about 10 more years. He said the college game served only as a training ground for the pros.

In a Dec. 5, 1940, article in the Kansas City Times, Allen also said he hoped basketball would never go "big time," and complained about that season's trip to New York and Philadelphia for road games in front of big crowds.

"If I had my way, we wouldn't go," he said. "I would rather stay at home in our own gym and work on fundamentals. That's where Big Six titles are won, working at home in the Christmas holidays. But the boys want a big trip. They always have, so finally they are getting one."

PHOG'S NEW GAME Allen invented "Goal High" in the summer of 1939. It was a variation of basketball using only one goal.

Two teams, each with five players, shot at the goal during their possession. The game included 2- and 3- point baskets, depending on where the ball was shot

The 1939-40 Kansas team, the NCAA Western Region champions, was captured in a number of photos with a western theme. Besides this "six-shooter shot" of the Big Six tri-champs, they were also photographed on horseback in full cowboy getup.

from on the floor. The 3-point line was from 15 feet out. The playing field was 30 feet in diameter.

Kansas won 22 consecutive games against Kansas State from Jan. 11, 1938, to Feb. 20, 1947.

1939-40: THE JAYHAWKS VS. THE "SUN-BRONZED GIANTS"

The Jayhawks finished the 1939-40 Big Six season at 8-2, in a three-way tie for the league title with Missouri and Oklahoma. A playoff series to determine who would represent the league in the Fifth District title game was held in Wichita. And KU prevailed, beating Oklahoma 45-39 after the Sooners had beaten Missouri.

In a contest billed as "The Game of the Year," Kansas met Oklahoma A&M for the Fifth District title. The Jayhawks won 45-43 in overtime and headed for the Western Championships in Kansas City.

After defeating Rice 50-44, KU advanced to meet Southern Cal in the NCAA Western final. The Jayhawks weren't given much of a chance: "The midget University of Kansas basketball team was up against the sun-bronzed giants rated the best in the nation. The Jayhawks looked puny in comparison," the Saturday Evening Post reported. But KU hung close and rallied in the final 18 seconds for a victory as Howard Engleman swished a high, arching shot from far out on the right side as the timer's gun went off. The Jayhawks had won 43-42. "It was another miracle in Kansas basketball. Kansas fans should be getting used to them by this time," the Post reported.

Bob "Junior" Allen, Phog's son, made the key steal and assist in the final seconds of the KU-USC game at the 1940 NCAA Western final. KU defeated the Trojans 43-42 and moved on to play Indiana in the NCAA final.

KU QUIZ

20. Who was KU's first three-time all-conference player?

21. Who were the Iron Five?

22. When Hoch Auditorium opened in 1927, what was it called?

But the miracles were over, and KU fell to Indiana 60-42 in the NCAA final at Kansas City's Municipal Auditorium. Dick Harp and Don Ebling were captains of the 1939-40 team. But other key players in Allen's "seven-man starting lineup" were Ralph Miller and Allen's son, Bob, who had fed Engleman the assist in the USC game.

PHOG'S FAVORITE: PART TWO

"The 1940 team ranks tops for their ability to overcome tremendous odds and advancing to the NCAA finals. …. In achieving national fame, this team owned no 'big men' yet had the necessary team work and qualifications to rank as one of the greatest K.U. teams of all time."

(Allen in the University Daily Kansan, December 1949)

TAKE THE TIE As far as Phog was concerned, a tie for the conference championship was as good as having solo honors in 1941:

"The doctor was jubilant today altho some of the rabid fans were nursing headaches after watching Oklahoma trim the Jayhawks, 45 to 37, last night.

"'I'm so pleased that we got as far as we did that it offsets everything else,' he continued. 'We have a tie for first, and all along I thought we'd get fourth. The future looks good, too; maybe that's why I'm happy. …

"'I'm very happy we aren't eligible for the N.C.A.A. play,' Allen said. 'Iowa State is a swell team and will go farther than we would have in the play-offs – if she is chosen by the committee.

"'Yes sir , I'm a very relieved man. My team is too small and too tired to partake of any post-season play , and besides, I want nothing to do with the N.C.A.A.'"

(Story in the Lawrence Journal-World, March 8, 1941)

TEACHING BY EXAMPLE

"A boy has to train to be on Phog's team. A few athletes have been dropped for violations. Phog never drinks or smokes. 'I've always been tempted by a cigar after dinner, and I don't think it would hurt me much,' he says, 'but I ask the boys not to, so…'

"Until a few years ago he would invite an athlete suspected of breaking training rules to the

HOMES OF THE JAYHAWKS

Thousands of fans pack into the monstrous Allen Fieldhouse each year to watch the Jayhawks play basketball. But KU's program had a more humble beginning.

KU's first home was in old Snow Hall. The court was 36 feet wide and 84 feet long. The ceiling was only 11 feet high, but it was later raised to 16 feet.

Fires destroyed two of KU's other early homes – 807 Kentucky Street, a skating rink where home games were played, and the Lawrence YMCA, which was KU's home until it burned down in 1902.

In 1907, KU had its first real home – Robinson Gymnasium, which was built for $100,000. Dr. James Naismith was heavily involved in the planning of the 3,000-seat gym.

KU's next home, Hoch Auditorium or "Horrendous Hoch," had a reputation for being one of the most difficult arenas to visit in the Midwest. But KU had great success in Hoch between 1928 and 1955, collecting 16 first-place conference finishes. Hoch,

which was destroyed by fire in 1991, was built for $350,000. It didn't have a home-team locker room, and KU teams would dress in nearby Robinson Gymnasium before games.

Allen Fieldhouse, named for legendary coach Phog Allen, opened its doors March 1, 1955. It was built for about $2.5 million and was the second-largest basketball arena in the nation at the time.

"In this hour of great recognition of my services to the University of Kansas, I feel very unworthy and deeply grateful," Allen said following word that the fieldhouse would be named in his honor. "No one can realize my feelings. I am just benumbed and overwhelmed."

KU defeated in-state rival Kansas State 77-67 in the fieldhouse's inaugural game. One-hundred and three former KU basketball lettermen were on hand for the dedication.

Allen Fieldhouse now seats 15,800, making it one of the largest on-campus playing arenas in the nation.

Allen's All-Americans

Paul Endacott, 1922, 1923

Charlie T. Black , 1923, 1924

Tusten Ackerman, 1924, 1925

Gale Gordon, 1925, 1926

Albert Peterson, 1925, 1926

Forrest Cox, 1930

Ted O'Leary, 1932

Bill Johnson, 1933

Ray Ebling, 1936

Fred Pralle, 1937, 1938

Howard Engleman, 1941

Ray Evans, 1942, 1943

Charlie B. Black, 1942, 1943, 1946, 1947

Clyde Lovellette, 1950, 1951, 1952

B.H. Born, 1953

gymnasium and beat him soundly in handball. Defeat from a grandfather was usually lesson enough for a prodigal youngster, without a word said. Several years ago, however, when his All-American forward, Ted O'Leary, got the invitation to the handball court, Ted trounced Phog soundly. Players have noticed a marked decrease in the frequency of handball invitations."

(Story in the Saturday Evening Post, Dec. 28, 1940)

THE PREGAME RITUAL The same article detailed Allen's pregame ritual:

1. At 3:20 in the afternoon, the boys report to a designated rooming house, where Phog puts them to bed "undressed and between clean sheets." They sleep for an hour and a half.

2. They get up and walk a mile.

3. They eat. Menu: half a grapefruit, a small cup of honey, two pieces of whole-wheat toast, half an order of celery and a cup of hot chocolate.

4. Next they warm their feet in front of a fireplace for about 15 minutes. "Get their feet warm," Phog says, "and the kids will calm down."

5. Take heated taxicabs to the arena 1 1/2 hours before the game.

6. Thirty minutes before the game, they have a shoot-around. But they only shoot short shots. If they make too many long shots during practice, according to Phog, they might get the idea that they can make them all the time, and try too many during the game.

7. Starters announced in locker room, pregame pep talk.

PUTTING THE DRIBBLE BACK IN BASKETBALL When the dribble was abolished in basketball, Allen became so angry that he quickly formed a meeting of coaches in Des Moines, Iowa, after the Drake Relays. Allen spread so much dissension toward the new rule that it was overturned, and the dribble was back in the game. From that protest, the National Association of Basketball Coaches was created, with Allen as the organization's first president.

1941-42: BACK IN THE NCAA

As the Jayhawks finished the 1941-42 Big Six season 8-2 and in a tie for first, Allen had clinched at least a

Phog Allen congratulates Ralph "Cappy" Miller after the KU-USC game at the 1940 NCAA Western Championship in Kansas City, Mo.

share of his 25th league title in 32 years of college coaching. KU again met Oklahoma A&M for the Fifth District NCAA final. Ralph Miller led KU with 17 points as the Jayhawks won 32-28. In the first round of the NCAA Western playoffs, KU lost to Colorado 46-44, despite Charlie B. Black's 18 points. In the consolation game, Black scored 16 as KU beat Rice 55-53. Black was named to the NCAA Western tournament team, and he and Evans were named All-Americans.

CAPPY MOVES ON Ralph "Cappy" Miller, who also lettered three years as a starting quarterback for KU, ended his Jayhawk career in 1942. After serving three years in the Air Force, Miller, who was from Chanute, Kan., went to coach at Wichita East High School, where he won a state championship before being named head coach at Wichita State. Fourteen years and 220 victories later, Miller moved on to Iowa for six years. He ended his career with 18 years at Oregon State. A two-time national Coach of the Year, Miller was named to the Naismith Hall of Fame in 1988 and retired after the 1989 season.

"GREATEST BASKETBALL COACH OF ALL TIME" In January 1943, Phog Allen was designated as "the greatest basket-

By 1945, Phog Allen was doing his part to keep former KU athletes fighting overseas in touch with the school and each other. He produced a newsletter called "Jayhawk Rebounds" with all the athletic news of the university to send to soldiers who had been players at KU. He also printed letters written to him from the soldiers and included their addresses so they could contact each other.

Phog Allen's Jayhawks had only two losing records in his 39 seasons at KU: 1928-29 (3-15 overall, 2-8 in Big Six) and 1947-48 (9-15 overall, 4-8 in Big Seven).

ball coach of all time" in the collegiate basketball record from the Helms Foundation of Los Angeles. The organization contacted coaches and basketball authorities across the country in conducting its survey.

"HOUDINI OF THE COURT" Allen called John Buescher, who played center for the Jayhawks for three seasons from 1941 to 1943, the "Houdini of basketball."

The March 7, 1943, Kansas City Star reported, "The K.U. mentor claims that Buescher can do almost everything except make the ball disappear on the court."

"THE QUIG" BECOMES A.D. E.C. Quigley became athletic director at Kansas in 1944, but he had been involved with the university's sports programs and with athletics around Lawrence for years.

Early game accounts often list Quigley as the official for KU basketball games, and he developed a cult following of KU students. If Quigley was officiating, the Kansan said, "that alone is worth the price of admission."

Quigley, a four-sport letterman, had played football at KU in 1900 and 1901. He became an official after suffering a broken hand playing professional baseball. Quigley estimated that in his 40-year career, he worked 400 football games, 5,400 major-league baseball games and 1,500 basketball games. He spent 23 years in the National League, worked AAU and NCAA basketball tournament games and the 1936 Olympic basketball finals. The KU baseball field is named after him, and he was elected to the Naismith Hall of Fame in 1961.

KU QUIZ

23. Who was the first KU player to play professional basketball?

CHARLIE BLACKS This Charlie Black thing can get downright confusing. That's because there were two at KU.

Charlie Black the First (Charles T.) played at KU from 1922 to 1924 and was captain of the 1924 team. He played on KU's two Helms Foundation championship teams.

Charlie Black the Second (Charles B.) lettered at KU in 1942 and '43, then left to fight in World War II before lettering again in 1946 and '47. He led the Big Six in scoring in 1945-46, averaging 17.3 points per game. He also was named All-Big Six and All-American in 1942, '43, '46 and '47, KU's only four-time All-American.

HEADED OVER THERE Several members of KU's 1942-43 team that finished 10-0 in the Big Six went off to war after the season, including Charlie Black, Armand Dixon, Ray Evans and Otto Schnellbacher. Their absence was obvious in the next season as KU fell to 17-9 overall and 5-5 in the Big Six.

ON THE UNDERCARD The Jan. 8, 1947, Lawrence Journal-World reported on a confrontation between Allen and Missouri coach Wilbur Stalcup at the game in Lawrence:

"Missouri won the basketball game with K.U. last night, and as an added attraction, heated words were exchanged near the close of the contest between the rival coaches, Dr. F.C. Allen and Wilbur Stalcup.

"With only a few minutes remaining in the game, Pleasant Smith, Tiger guard, committed his fifth foul of the game. Stalcup rushed out on the court protesting the decision and shouting at the officials.

"Coach F.C. Allen arose from the Kansas bench and walked along the side of the playing court to Stalcup and said, 'Why don't you get off the court and stay on the bench.'

"At no time did Allen lay a hand on the Missouri coach. Stalcup told Allen in no uncertain terms to get back on his side of the court and stay there. Just as Allen was turning away, Stalcup

They had the same name, played the same game and went to the same school. But the two Charlie Blacks played at different times at KU. At left, Charlie T. Black, who played in the 1920s. At right, Charlie B. Black, who played in the 1940s.

raised his arm and pushed the veteran Kansas mentor. Allen did not turn around but kept right on going to the Kansas bench.

"Allen said this morning that his only intent in protesting to Stalcup was to call the attention of the officials to the fact that the Missouri mentor was violating a rule. The rules say that no coach or player shall go onto the court without first being recognized by the officials."

PHOG TAKES A REST Allen missed the end of the 1946-47 season when the university granted him an indefinite leave, allowing him to recuperate from a bout with influenza. Allen also reportedly had suffered dizzy spells and severe headaches after receiving a concussion during a practice earlier in the season.

He spent his time resting in California.

Assistant coach Howard Engleman led the team to an 8-6 record while Allen was getting his R & R.

BIG MAN ON CAMPUS Clyde Lovellette, all 6 feet 10 inches of him, arrived at KU in 1948. Lovellette, who suffered from a slight case of asthma, took Allen's advice to attend KU, the Kansas City Star reported:

"'Up here on the hill a tall man can stand up

By 1943, many KU players were trading in their basketball uniforms for military garb. These players were inducted to the Army in March 1943 (from left to right): Hoyt Baker, Don Blair, Bill Brill, George Dick, Armand Dixon and Ray Evans.

straight and breathe the rarified atmosphere,' says Phog. It was that advice to Lovellette ... which resulted in the 18-year-old basketball player coming to K.U. from Terre Haute, Ind. It has made a number of Hoosier coaches unhappy."

BEFORE THERE WAS GATORADE ...

"In the fury of the game, Phog consumes water like a steam engine. He keeps the players' water bottles at his feet. Every few seconds he reaches down and takes a swig. He says a moist pharnyx keeps down nervousness, and if that is true, he needs plenty of moistening. He bleeds when his team is out there playing. ...

"By the time the final gun goes off, Phog has consumed about six quarts of water."

(Story in the Saturday Evening Post, Dec. 28, 1940)

A FLICK, THEN A PUNCH

"Dr. Phog Allen, Kansas basketball coach, 'ducked a wild right haymaker' tossed by Referee Eddie Davidson in a hubbub that arose in the K.U.-Washington University basketball game at St. Louis Saturday night after Sonny Enns, Jayhawk cager, 'flicked the official on the nose with his fingers.' That was the K.U. coach's version of the affair today of what a St. Louis newspaper described as a 'near riot.' Kansas and Washington resumed basketball after a 21-year lay-off with the Jayhawkers claiming a 46 to 41 victory."

Allen told the Kansas City Star about the Jan. 15, 1949, game, saying that the referee, Al Davidson, charged the Kansas bench after being struck in the face by the basketball when a KU player tossed it to him after a foul.

KU QUIZ

24. What was Ralph "Cappy" Miller's other popular nickname?

"'Apparently Referee Davidson erroneously supposed the ball was thrown from our bench. ... I stood up from the bench so that I could better understand his statements. He was protesting, and while he stood there so doing, Sonny Enns, who was standing next to me, flicked Referee Davidson on the nose with his fingers.

"'Apparently Referee Davidson thought I was the guilty individual because he unloosed a wild right haymaker in the direction of my head.'

"Allen ducked the punch, and KU's reserve players and the other official helped restrain Davidson.

Jayhawk mainstays from the 1951-52 championship season (from left to right): Bob Kenney, Bill Hougland, Clyde Lovellette, Bill Lienhard and Charlie Hoag.

"Allen said, 'I shifted to one side, allowing the blow to pass on. I had my glasses on and did not care to receive the referee's retaliation on so vulnerable a spot.'"

1951-52: GREATEST EVER?

Allen had recruited his 1951-52 team members with the promise that they would be the squad to represent the United States in the '52 Olympics. He had reason to be confident in that prediction, knowing Lovellette would be playing his senior season.

And Lovellette's supporting staff was stellar, as well. Bob "Trigger" Kenney ended his college career as the nation's best free-throw shooter. His career average of 79.1 percent still ranks among KU's top 10. There was also 5-11 Dean Kelley, a defensive whiz; junior Charlie Hoag, the team's "sparkplug;" Bill Lienhard, described as "the finest one-hand set-shot artist in Kansas basketball history;" Bill Hougland, who picked up the slack when Lovellette got in foul trouble; and John Keller, who moved from being Lovellette's backup to a starting forward.

The Jayhawks rolled to an 11-1 record for the Big Seven title, falling only to Kansas State, 81-64 at Manhattan. When KU won the rematch in Lawrence, the Jayhawks moved into the league lead for good and Allen evened his career rivalry with K-State coach Jack

Gardner at 10 wins apiece.

KU also won its first Big Seven tournament crown.

One of the season's biggest wins, however, came against Henry Iba's Oklahoma A&M (later Oklahoma State). The Aggies had beaten KU in the teams' first meeting, 49-45, KU's only other regular-season loss. But when they met in Lawrence on Feb. 19, the Jayhawks won 66-46, giving Allen his 700th career victory, more than 100 ahead of any contemporary.

KU met Texas Christian in the first round of the NCAA Regional in Kansas City and won 68-64 after leading TCU by as many as 17 points late in the game. Next up was St. Louis, and Lovellette exploded for an NCAA tournament single-game record 44 points to take KU from a 27-27 halftime tie to a 74-55 rout in the regional final.

Lovellette stayed hot, scoring 33 points as KU beat Santa Clara 74-55 in the NCAA semifinals in Seattle, setting up the championship game against St. John's.

Lovellette again scored 33 points, and Bill Lienhard and Robert Kenney added 12 apiece as the Jayhawks romped 80-63. KU had won its first NCAA championship in what was, at that time, the most lopsided final in tournament history.

And the season was not over. KU went back to Kansas City to face the Springfield Missouri State Teachers (later Southwest Missouri State) in the first round of the Olympic playoffs. The Jayhawks won 92-65, establishing a new single-game scoring record. The NIT champion, LaSalle, was next, and KU won 70-65 in the semifinals at Madison Square Garden as Lovellette scored 40 points.

The win over LaSalle had assured the Jayhawks of

Clyde Lovellette's top five scoring games

1952: vs. St. Louis, 44 points

1952: vs. Southern Methodist, 42 points

1952: vs. Colorado, 41 points

1952: vs. LaSalle, 40 points

1950: vs. Missouri, 39 points

The 1952 Olympic team included seven members of KU's NCAA championship squad. Pictured kneeling (from left to right): Dean Kelley, Charlie Hoag, John Keller, Bob Kenney, Bill Hougland, Bill Lienhard and Clyde Lovellette. Phog Allen, who was an assistant coach, is standing far left.

KU's Bill Hougland joined his teammates to capture a gold medal in the 1952 Olympics in Helsinki. But it wasn't his only gold. He was also a member of the 1956 Olympic team that won gold in Melbourne.

In 1952, a grass-roots movement came about to elect Phog Allen president as an independent candidate. It was started by K-State coach Jack Gardner, who drew up the petition after watching KU's 1952-53 team practice. "I want to see Phog Allen any place but coaching in the Big Seven next season," Gardner said. Allen replied that Gardner "would do anything to get rid of me."

placing seven players on the Olympic squad, and KU met AAU champion Peoria Caterpillar-Diesels in the Olympic finals to determine who would coach the team in Helsinki. Peoria won in the final eight seconds when Howie Williams, a former Purdue guard, hit a short jumper to break a 60-60 tie. Peoria coach Warren Womble was named the Olympic coach, and Allen was named an assistant.

Allen had kept his promise. The seven Jayhawks on the Olympic team that won the gold medal in Helsinki were: Lovellette, Kenney, Kelley, Lienhard, Hougland, Hoag and Keller.

"CUMULOUS" CLYDE WRAPS IT UP Lovellette, a country boy from Terre Haute who had been intent on playing for Indiana, had come to KU because Allen promised to build a championship team around him. He did, and Lovellette shattered most KU records in the process. A two-time All-American, he set an NCAA Tournament record of 141 points and was named the 1952 NCAA tourney's MVP. He is KU's second all-time scorer with 1,888 points, an average of 24.5 points a game. During his senior season, Lovellette led the nation with a 28.4 point average.

After KU, Lovellette played one year with the Phillips 66ers in the AAU, then 12 years in the NBA at Minneapolis, Cincinnati, St. Louis and Boston. He played on three NBA championship teams: the 1954 Lakers and the 1963 and '64 Celtics.

He retired from the NBA in 1964 and was elected to the Naismith Hall of Fame in 1988.

1952-53: ALMOST A REPEAT

The Jayhawks had almost been expected to be national champs in 1952, but no one thought they'd get close the next year. After KU lost to Rice in the second game of the season, there were predictions that the Jayhawks would be lucky to win five games.

So when KU came within one basket of another NCAA title in March, veteran Jayhawk observer Don Pierce called 1952-53 the "most astounding basketball season in Mt. Oread Annals."

With Lovellette gone, junior center B.H. Born emerged as the Jayhawks' leader, and he led the Big Seven with a 22.5 point average. Dean Kelley returned as the only starter from the 1952 team and served as captain as the Jayhawks finished 10-2 to take the conference title. They advanced to the Southwest Regional in Manhattan, Kan., and, led by Gil Reich's 20 points and Al Kelley's 17, beat Oklahoma City in the first round.

That set up another meeting with Hank Iba's Oklahoma A&M. The Aggies were ranked sixth in the nation, a notch behind KU, and featured a typically stingy defense and ball-control offense. KU had taken an 11-point lead early in the fourth quarter when Born fouled out. A&M took advantage of his loss and pulled to 57-55 but got no closer as KU stalled in the final minutes of the game for a 61-55 victory. Born scored 18 points, and Dean Kelley added 16, 10 of them in the third quarter while KU built up its lead.

The Final Four in Kansas City pitted KU against the Washington Huskies, the No.-2 ranked team in the country. Washington – led by All-American center Bob Houbregs, who averaged 25.4 points a game – was a four-point favorite going into the game.

KU QUIZ

25. What was significant about B.H. Born's 1953 NCAA Tournament performance?

B.H. Born emerged from Clyde Lovellette's shadow to lead KU to the 1953 NCAA final. Born, from Medicine Lodge, Kan., led the Jayhawks in scoring with a 22.5 point average.

B. H. BORN
All-American—1953
All Big Seven—1953-54

The 1952-53 Jayhawks made an unexpected return to the NCAA title game and came within one basket of repeating as champions. Above, the Big Seven champions are all smiles after winning their final conference game of the season, at Missouri.

But KU held Houbregs to 18 as the 6-foot-9 center, hampered by four fouls from the second quarter on, fouled out for the first time in 58 games.

Born, fighting a cold and often double-teamed, scored 25 points. Dean Kelley added 18 and Harold Patterson 17 as KU routed Washington 79-53 to advance to the final. Washington coach Tippy Dye was impressed, saying the Jayhawks "work harder at winning a basketball game than any team I've seen."

Hard work wasn't enough in the final against Indiana. KU led the game by as many as six points on two occasions, but Born fouled out with more than five minutes remaining. Both teams missed easy shots in the closing minutes, and KU tied the game with 1:19 remaining. But the Jayhawks fouled Don Leonard with 27 seconds remaining, and he made what was the winning free throw. KU's Jerry Alberts watched his desperation shot from the corner hit the front of the rim as the buzzer sounded. Indiana had held on for a 69-68 victory.

But the Jayhawks had put together a stunningly successful season, and none more so than Born. He had scored 51 points and collected 20 rebounds in the two Final Four games and was named an All-American.

Not bad for a guy who averaged 1.6 points per game the season before as a backup center.

TAKIN' NOTES Another member of both the 1951-52 and

1952-53 teams was Dean Smith, who was from Emporia, Kan. He was a little-used reserve forward who apparently made valuable use of his time on the sidelines, paying close attention to how to win games. Smith went on to coaching fame at North Carolina, leading the Tar Heels to NCAA titles in 1982 and 1993. Heading into the 1993-94 season, he had taken his UNC teams to 18 straight NCAA Tournaments and 10 trips to the Final Four. UNC had won 20 or more games for 23 straight seasons and his 774 career victories surpassed Allen. He was inducted to the Naismith Hall of Fame in 1984.

Guess he was paying attention.

KU QUIZ

26. What was Dean Smith's college nickname?

THE STUDENT MEETS THE TEACHER On Dec. 7, 1955, Allen and his Jayhawks met a Wichita State team coached by former KU standout Ralph Miller. Miller had exploded for 30 points against the Wheatshockers back in 1942

Dean Smith (center, facing the camera) pays close attention to Phog Allen's pregame speech before the championship matchup against St. John's in the 1952 NCAA final.

when the two teams had met in Wichita's old Forum.

But the 1955 matchup was being played to dedicate WSU's new Levitt Arena, and Miller was hoping to upset his former team, even though the Wheatshockers hadn't beaten KU in four previous meetings. Playing without two starters, KU still beat WSU 56-55. Miller went on to coach at Iowa and Oregon State and retired in 1989 after 39 years in college coaching.

BIGGER MAN ON CAMPUS The main attraction for the 1955-56 season never suited up for a varsity game. Seven-footer Wilton Chamberlain, ineligible as a freshman, had chosen KU over LaSalle, Indiana and Illinois and created a furor when he arrived in Lawrence.

More than 14,000 people packed Allen Fieldhouse to watch Wilt's freshman team defeat the varsity 81-71. Chamberlain scored 42 points, only two shy of Lovellette's scoring record, which Wilt later shattered.

RULES ARE RULES With the exception of the excitement created by Chamberlain, the 1955-56 season was a disappointing one for Allen and the Jayhawks. KU went 6-6 in the Big Seven, its second straight fifth-place finish, and was 14-9 overall.

With Chamberlain on campus, all talk centered on the 1956-57 season, and Allen, understandably, wanted to be a part of it.

The night Wilt scored 42 points for the freshmen against the varsity was Allen's birthday, but not

The 1955-56 Kansas team was the last team Phog Allen coached. It was also the first team to play a full season in Allen Fieldhouse, which was named after Allen. In the nine games played in the fieldhouse that year, the Jayhawks won seven.

necessarily a joyous occasion. He had reached the state's mandatory retirement age of 70 and was scheduled to retire June 1, 1956.

He didn't go without a fight.

Allen appealed the decision all the way to the Board of Regents, even offering to give up his teaching duties if he could keep his coaching job. But the state wouldn't budge, and he coached his final game on March 10, 1956, a conference game against Colorado in Boulder. The Jayhawks lost 75-67.

"This season was disappointing," he said.

"It would be the thrill of my life to end a long coaching career with a truly great team."

In 1972, his comments were even stronger.

"I wanted just one more year. I wanted to coach Wilt Chamberlain with those 10-foot baskets. I was going to make them swallow those baskets."

Dick Harp

Years Coached at KU: 1956-64
KU Record: 121-82, .596 winning percentage

Dick Harp, longtime assistant to Phog Allen and a former Kansas player, was faced with following a living legend when he took over as KU's head coach after Allen's forced retirement in 1956.

Harp hadn't even applied to be an assistant under Allen in the first place. He had lettered three years as a guard for KU and was co-captain of the 1939-40 team that lost to Indiana in the NCAA final. He then served 4 ½ years as a master sergeant in the Army during World War II. He was working in Kansas City while going to law school and coaching basketball part-time at William Jewell College in Liberty, Mo., when Allen asked him to return to KU in 1949.

The head coaching job came with some perks in 1956 – Wilt Chamberlain, the 7-foot phenom, was eligible to play after sitting out his freshman year. KU's 1956-57 season was Harp's finest as the Jayhawks advanced to the NCAA championship game, making Harp one of only five people to have coached and played in the final.

Under Harp, Chamberlain and forward Bill Bridges earned All-American honors and the Jayhawks earned two conference titles and two NCAA berths.

Harp resigned as head coach in 1964. A deeply religious man, he went to work for the Fellowship of Christian Athletes in June 1964 and retired as senior vice president of the organization in March 1983. He accepted a position as Dean Smith's administrative assistant at North Carolina in 1986 and worked there until 1989. He still lives in Lawrence.

Wilt 52, It's All True

(Headline in the Kansas City Star, Dec. 4, 1956)

1956-57: HIGH HOPES

Wilt the Stilt (who preferred the nickname Big Dipper) caused a big stir at KU before he ever suited up for the varsity. Jayhawk fans couldn't wait to see their 7-foot center in action.

He did not disappoint.

In Chamberlain's first varsity game, an 87-69 drubbing of Northwestern in Lawrence, he scored 52 points and grabbed 31 rebounds – both new school records – in front of 15,000 fans. He hit 20 of 29 field goals, mostly on dunk shots, and could have scored even more if he'd bettered his 12-of-20 mark from the free-throw line. The 52 points still stand as a KU single-game record, although Chamberlain broke the rebound mark when he collected 36 against Iowa State in 1958. Phog Allen, who had recruited Chamberlain, was not in the stands to see Wilt's varsity debut, having traveled out of town for one of his many speaking engagements.

Before the opening of the 1955 fall semester at KU, university housing officials were obviously confident that Chamberlain would show up on campus, the Kansan reported on Dec. 4, 1956. They had ordered a specially constructed 7 1/2 foot bed for the Philadelphia recruit.

But the other KU fans on hand saw just what they expected from Chamberlain, and according to the March 1957 Alumni Magazine, "Many expected the team to go through its season undefeated."

Not quite.

After 12 straight wins, the Jayhawks fell 39-37 to Iowa State, a last-second defeat at Ames. In its next game, KU beat ISU 75-64 in Lawrence in a game much more suited to the Jayhawks' tempo. After four more wins, KU lost 56-54 to Oklahoma State, again on a last-second shot. Henry Iba's Aggies taught the Jayhawks "the danger of a pressure defense by a fine team," according to the Alumni Magazine.

But the Jayhawks were developing into a championship-caliber team. Four veterans had begun the year in the starting lineup with Wilt: Gene Elstun, Lew Johnson, Maurice King and John Parker. At the semester break, Ron Loneski moved into Johnson's place as a starter. Loneski had broken a bone in his foot in the first game of the season and had missed more than a month of the season.

The Jayhawks also switched at mid-year from man-to-man to zone defense, in order to take advantage of KU's size for rebounding, Harp said.

After closing out the conference season with four more victories to finish 11-1 and clinch the Big Seven title, KU headed to the NCAA regional in Dallas.

The Jayhawks' first-round opponent was Southern Methodist, the host school. SMU had won 35 straight games at home and played tough against the Jayhawks, but KU won 73-65 in overtime. The Jayhawks met Oklahoma City in the regional final and rolled to an 81-61 victory.

At the Final Four in Kansas City, KU made quick work of San Francisco, winning 80-56 to set up the championship game against No. 1-ranked North

Carolina.

27. Dick Harp also was connected with the KU football program. How?

28. Wilt Chamberlain later built a $1.5 million "paradise pad" near Los Angeles when he played for the Lakers. What did he call it?

THE FINAL On March 23, 1957, KU and North Carolina met in one of the most thrilling championship games in NCAA history.

The Jayhawks trailed 29-22 at the half, but they battled back to force the game into overtime – the first of three extra periods. With six seconds remaining in the third OT, the Tar Heels, coached by Frank McGuire, led the Jayhawks 54-53. KU had the ball out of bounds at half court, and everyone knew what was coming: Wilt was going to get the ball.

Johnny Parker threw the ball in to Ron Loneski, who dribbled a couple of times before throwing a soft pass high to Chamberlain. But North Carolina center Joe Quigg jumped in front of Chamberlain and deflected the ball to teammate Tommy Kearns, who heaved the ball high into the rafters as the buzzer sounded.

Chamberlain and the Jayhawks finished the season 24-3, with a second-place trophy to show for it.

"The best team won," Harp said afterward. "They deserved to win it. They had the determination to win."

And before the mob of press surged into the locker room, the Topeka Capitol-Journal reported, Harp said, "This is the happiest year of my life, even though it says second place on the trophy."

But Wilt didn't view it so positively, and in his autobiography he later wrote about the game:

"I've always been more bitter about that loss than almost any other single game in my whole college and professional career."

THE MORE THINGS CHANGE ... According to the February 1958 Alumni Magazine, Harp kept in place most of Phog Allen's pregame ritual. The team still spent the afternoon napping at the Eldridge Hotel and ate a light dinner of toast, honey, celery and tea at the Jayhawk Cafe before heading to the fieldhouse.

THEY GET AROUND The demands on the 1956-57 team went beyond basketball, according to the Alumni Magazine. Blaine Hollinger was one of KU's Rhodes Scholar candidates. He flew with the team to Seattle for its western swing early in the season, flew back to Des Moines, Iowa, for Rhodes Scholar interviews and then rejoined the team in California. Two months later, he helped KU's track team to a Big Seven indoor title by winning the broad jump before flying to Boulder to join the basketball team in its game against Colorado.

Chamberlain also had a harried schedule. He averaged two interview sessions a week with national media and appeared on TV's "The Ed Sullivan Show." In order to appear with the Associated Press All-America team, he rushed to Kansas City after scoring 40 points in KU's final conference game, flew to New York and then flew back in time for classes Monday. He repeated the trip after the NCAA championship game to make an appearance with the Look All-America team.

NICE GUYS FINISH THIRD Harp and Chamberlain agreed early in the 1956-57 season that they would not leave the 7-footer in a game just to run up his scoring average when an opponent was obviously defeated. According to the March 1957 Alumni Magazine, the rule of thumb was that Wilt could stay in the game as long as KU was fewer than 20 points ahead. There were two exceptions, both against Colorado: in the conference preseason tournament, when the players asked that Wilt be allowed to break the tournament scoring record; and in the final conference game of the season, when Wilt was left in to give all the players a chance to play with him.

Chamberlain finished third in the national scoring race, missing first by a little more than one point a game.

PHOG SAYS On May 6, 1957, Allen was quoted in a wire story as saying that Wilt would "definitely" turn pro and

Dick Harp and his assistant, former KU player Jerry Waugh, far left, found themselves in charge on the sidelines for KU's 1956-57 season.

*Wilt's Top 10
Scoring Games*

'57 vs. Northwestern,
52 points

'58 vs. Nebraska, 46

'57 vs. Colorado, 45

'58 vs. Oklahoma, 41

'57 vs. Colorado, 40

'58 vs. Marquette, 40

'57 vs. Marquette, 39

'58 vs. K-State, 38

'57 vs. Washington,
37

'58 vs. Washington,
37

not return for his junior season: "Why, Wilt made more than $100,000 for the University of Kansas last year. He thinks it is time he made a little for himself."

The same day, Chamberlain said he found the comments interesting: "It would appear that Phog knows more about my business than I do." All Chamberlain would say was, "Nobody knows what may happen between now and September."

1957-58: HE'S BACK

Chamberlain did return for his junior season at KU. But his veteran supporting cast of Elstun, King, Johnson and Parker had graduated. Even with Wilt's average of 30.1 points a game (still a KU record for single-season average), KU finished 18-5 overall and 8-4 for a second-place tie in the conference and failed to qualify for the NCAA Tournament.

But the season was not without its highlights. On Feb. 8 in Lawrence, KU met Nebraska, which was stuck in the league cellar. Behind Chamberlain's 46 points, which broke B.H. Born's conference record of 44, the Jayhawks beat the Cornhuskers 104-46. The total broke KU's previous scoring record of 100 points, set against Rice in the 1954-55 season.

And in the final game of the season, KU met K-State, the conference champion and No. 1-ranked team in the nation. Chamberlain, in his final game as a Jayhawk, scored 24 points as the Jayhawks controlled the game throughout, beating the Wildcats 61-44 in Manhattan.

ON THE AIR ... Chamberlain, who was a radio and TV major, had his own radio show, "Flip'er with Dipper," at the student radio station. The 30-minute show featured rhythm and blues music.

... AND CUTTING SOME VINYL Wilt made a record in 1960 and then appeared on Dick Clark's "American Bandstand."

"The squealers almost lost their squeals when Wilt broke into a stylish shuffle. He was as graceful as he is when he leaps skyward and dunks two points through the hoops," the Associated Press reported.

The record, which Wilt said he released to stop his parents and siblings from laughing at his singing, featured the songs "By the River" and "That's Easy to Say."

A TEAM PLAYER After he scored only a few points against Colorado during a game in 1958, the University Daily

Kansan had this observation about Chamberlain:

"What makes a basketball player, in hot pursuit of the national scoring title, pass up a chance to score 35 or 40 points and settle for six?...

"The answer, to those who were in Boulder Monday night, is simple. Wilt is a team man. To him the most important thing is a victory for Kansas – national scoring titles or records are second in his book. ...

"Jayhawker coach Dick Harp: 'Wilt has virtually destroyed his chance to win the national scoring crown because of his play Monday night. I never knew anyone unselfish enough to do this sort of thing. This just proves Wilt is a fine playmaker and a fine team man. This was all his own idea.'"

TIGER FOOD Following a KU victory in Missouri in the 1957-58 season, longtime Jayhawk observer Don Pierce

Wilt Chamberlain, shown taking one of his vintage high-percentage shots, was the complete basketball package. He combined size with grace to dominate at both the college and pro levels.

reported that not even a "fanging from the Tigers slowed down the Kansas towerhouse as he crammed home the second-highest total a Brewer Fieldhouse visitor ever scored at 35."

"'Tell 'em,' Wilt Chamberlain said, holding aloft a left arm with two rows of teeth marks clearly etched on the forearm, 'that if they're short of food over here we'll supply 'em with some. Somebody tried to bite the heck out of me.'"

WILT HITS THE ROAD After two seasons with the Jayhawks, Chamberlain left the university, skipping his senior year of eligibility. He left town and headed to Philadelphia in May 1958 in a new red convertible, a bonus payment from the Harlem Globetrotters after he agreed to play one year on their exhibition tour.

Because of NCAA rules, Wilt was ineligible to play in the NBA until after his college eligibility had ended. He eventually entered the NBA with the Philadelphia Warriors in 1959 and retired in 1973 as the league's second all-time leading scorer with 31,419 points. He was a four-time MVP and set a single-game record when he scored 100 points against the New York Knicks on March 2, 1962. He was named to the Naismith Hall of Fame in 1978.

Chamberlain told the Lawrence Journal-World on May 23, 1958: "If I had to start over again from high school, I would want to attend the University of Kansas. ...

Wilt's Top 10 Rebounding Games

'58 vs. ISU, 36 rebounds

'57 vs. Northwestern, 31

'57 vs. Washington, 28

'58 vs. Missouri, 27

'57 vs. Wisconsin, 24

'57 vs. Iowa State, 24

'57 vs. Iowa State, 24

'58 vs. Washington, 22

'57 vs. Marquette, 22

'57 vs. Missouri, 22

"I am sorry I have let some of these fine people down, but I just have to do this for me. It's what I feel is best."

The big-time money of professional basketball and the chance to escape the sagging zone defenses that had pounded on him during his collegiate career lured Chamberlain away from KU.

Wilt criticized the defensive tactics used by KU's opponents when explaining his decision to leave in a 1958 article in Look magazine: "The game I was forced to play at KU wasn't basketball. It was hurting my chances of ever developing into a successful professional player."

1959-60: WINNING WITHOUT WILT

The 1958-59 season without Chamberlain was a tough one for the Jayhawks, who finished 11-14 overall and 8-6 in the Big Eight for a third-place tie. But by the 1959-60 season, forwards Bill Bridges and Wayne Hightower had started to fill the gap. Hightower led the

The Big Dipper,
Wilt Chamberlain

KU QUIZ

29. Bill Bridges, an All-American in 1961, still ranks second in one KU statistical category. What is it?

Big Eight in scoring, averaging 21.6 points per game, as KU and K-State finished the conference season with 10-4 records. The two teams split their regular-season games against each other.

On March 9, the two met in Manhattan for a one-game playoff to determine the Big Eight's representative to the NCAA regional, which also was going to be held in Manhattan. K-State rallied to send the game to overtime, where KU won 84-82. Hightower had 28 points and guard Jerry Gardner scored 21 to lead the Jayhawks.

Two nights later, KU beat Texas 90-81 to advance to the regional final against No. 1 Cincinnati. But the pressure-filled games that closed KU's regular season and the NCAA opener had taken their toll on the Jayhawks. The Lawrence Journal-World reported on KU's 82-71 loss:

"With six players going most of the way, Kansas just didn't have the gas Saturday to go the entire

Forward Bill Bridges lettered from 1959 to 1961 and was a 1961 All-American. He stands No. 25 on KU's all-time scoring list.

route against classy Cincinnati and the great Oscar Robertson."

Hightower and Bridges scored 22 points each, but Robertson had 43 for the Bearcats. KU led 57-51 with 13:45 remaining in the game but allowed Cincy to tie it at 63 with 8:10 to go. The Jayhawks managed only eight more points as the Bearcats pulled away.

"I couldn't move near the end," Hightower told the Journal-World. "I just wore out."

Bridges and Hightower returned for the 1960-61 season, and Bridges was named All-American for that season. But KU didn't return to the NCAA Tournament during Harp's tenure.

In 1961-62, KU fell to 7-18 overall and 3-11 in the conference, tying for seventh place. It was the most losses in a season in KU history and the lowest a KU team would finish in the conference standings until 1983.

Wayne Hightower led KU in scoring in 1959-60 (21.8 points a game) and 1960-61 (20.7 points a game).

KU ON PROBATION The NCAA slapped the KU basketball and football programs with probation in October 1960.

The NCAA charged that in 1957 KU boosters had purchased a used car valued at $1,564 for Wilt Chamberlain. KU was ruled ineligible for postseason play for two seasons. Chamberlain called the allegation "ridiculous."

Kansas became the first school to be penalized for infractions in two sports at the same time. The football program had been penalized for a separate infraction.

WILT AND CLYDE Clyde Lovellette, with the St. Louis Hawks, and Wilt Chamberlain, with the Philadelphia Warriors, clashed on Oct. 10, 1960, at Allen Fieldhouse. The game gave Lovellette, who had played his regular-season games in Hoch Auditorium, an opportunity to play in the 17,000-seat fieldhouse.

The big guys put on a good show during their KU homecoming. Wilt scored 25 points and tipped in a shot with 20 seconds remaining to lead Philadelphia to a 104-103 victory. Lovellette also had a strong showing, scoring 21 points.

BAD BLOOD A brawl during the Kansas-Missouri game on national television in 1961 put the future of the rivalry in jeopardy.

"I feel that if this extreme bitterness continues between the two schools, we will have to discontinue playing each other, at least for a while," Athletic Director "Dutch" Lonborg told the Lawrence Journal-World.

The brawl reportedly began after KU's Wayne Hightower took a swing at MU's Charlie Henke after being fouled by him. Players from both teams and spectators got involved in the scuffle.

LOST TO THE PROS Wayne Hightower, who followed Wilt Chamberlain to KU from Philadelphia, left the team after the 1961 season to turn pro. Hightower said the decision was influenced by financial obligations, but others reported that the 6-foot-9 forward was having academic difficulty and in all likelihood would have been ineligible for the following basketball season.

HARP STEPS DOWN

KU had all-conference players in Nolen Ellison and George Unseld for the 1962-63 and 1963-64 seasons but finished no better than sixth and third, respectively, in

George Unseld led the Jayhawks in rebounding in 1962-63 and 1963-64. KU also recruited his brother, Wes, who later was an All-American at Louisville.

the Big Eight.

After a mid-season loss to K-State, Harp was hanged and burned in effigy on campus. The Jayhawks won five of their final eight games to finish 13-12 overall and 8-6 in the Big Eight.

But the season-ending rally was not enough.

After a 21-year relationship with Kansas basketball as either a player or a coach, Dick Harp left the university.

"I have determined that it is time for me to retire from coaching," Harp said in announcing his resignation. "My association with the University of Kansas has been a wonderful experience."

Harp said he had considered the decision all season and left with no bitterness.

"From the time I was a little boy, the biggest thing in my life was the University of Kansas," Harp told the Topeka Capital-Journal. "If I had to draw a pattern, I would draw it again. I was at Kansas as a player and coach. What more could I ask?

"The fact that it's time to change jobs doesn't alter that."

Soon after Harp's announcement, KU players circulated a petition unanimously calling for assistant Ted Owens to be hired. KU alums Ralph Miller and Dean Smith were also rumored to have been candidates for the job.

KU QUIZ

30. The 1961-62 team went 7-18, the most losses in school history. The mark was later tied by what team?

31. KU had back-to-back losing seasons in 1961-62 and 1962-63. Who was coach when the Jayhawks previously had done that?

Ted Owens

Years Coached at KU: 1964-1983
KU Record: 348-182, .657 winning percentage

Ted Owens, named the head basketball coach at KU on March 27, 1964, climbed aboard an emotional roller coaster he would ride until 1983. He led KU to the heights of two Final Four appearances and the depths of the school's first back-to-back losing seasons in a decade. Along the way, there was talk of lifetime contracts as well as fairly organized efforts to oust him from his job.

But Owens grabbed the bar and hung on tight for 19 years, a tenure at KU second only to Phog Allen's. The 348 victories he collected at KU also rank second only to Allen's 590.

Owens, who lettered three years with the University of Oklahoma basketball team, started his coaching career at Cameron State Junior College in Lawton, Okla., where his teams never won fewer than 20 games and three times advanced to the national junior-college tournament semifinals. Owens then became an assistant under KU's Dick Harp in 1960.

KU won six Big Eight titles under Owens and went to

Ted Owens was a fresh-faced young man of 34 when he took over the KU program after the 1963-64 season.

the NCAA Tournament seven times. The 1971 and 1974
KU teams advanced to the Final Four. He was named Big
Eight Coach of the Year five times and was Basketball
Weekly's national Coach of the Year in 1978.

Five All-Americans played under Owens: Jo Jo White,
Darnell Valentine, Dave Robisch, Bud Stallworth and
Walt Wesley.

WE WANT TED Soon after Dick Harp announced his
resignation, KU players signed a petition calling for
Owens to receive the head coaching job. The seniors on
the upcoming team, led by all-conference center George
Unseld, started the drive. The petition was then given to
KU Chancellor W. Clarke Wescoe.

THEY GET HIM The 34-year-old Owens was announced as
the KU coach in March 1964.

"To find myself as head basketball coach at the finest
basketball school in the country gives you a feeling
that is hard to describe," Owens told the Topeka
Capital-Journal. "Elation is hardly a word to describe
my feeling."

Owens, who was known as a top recruiter, got busy
on his new job – even before the announcement was
made that it was his. He was late to the news conference
introducing him as the head coach because he had been
meeting with a junior-college prospect, Al Lopes of
Coffeyville.

HARD WORK PAYS OFF Owens took his head coaching
debut in 1964 pretty seriously. Owens later recalled his
first game as KU head coach in a Wichita Eagle story:

"KU opened the (1964-65) season at Arkansas.
Owens tried to prepare his team like it was for the
national championship.

"'We were working twice a day, Saturdays and
Sundays, too,' he said. 'I was trying to get everything in.'

"He even called Glen Rose, then the Arkansas
coach, at home to see if he could get practice time
on the school's court the day before the game.

"'Glen isn't here,' Rose's wife said. 'He's out
fishing. They aren't even practicing today.'"

The Jayhawks won 65-60.

THOUGHT WE WERE IN LAWRENCE A conspiracy by a K-
State loyalist, known as the Wildcatman, left a capacity
crowd in Allen Fieldhouse stunned in February 1965

Jo Jo White, who led KU in scoring in 1967-68 (15.3 ppg), is No. 14 on the KU career scoring list with 1,286 points.

KU QUIZ

34. How did Jo Jo White get his nickname?

during a KU-K-State game. Sports Illustrated reported that the Wildcatman hid in a closet in the fieldhouse the night before the game "and contrived a complicated electrical device that triggered two huge signs into falling over the scoreboard in the very midst of the game. The signs read, "GO STATE: KILL SNOB HILL AGAIN."

The scoreboard was lowered at halftime and the banners were removed.

JO JO HYPE In the Jan. 24, 1966, Sports Illustrated, Frank Deford wrote about Jo Jo White, who would join the Jayhawks at midterm:

> "The freshman Jayhawks were led by a 6-foot-3 guard, Jo-Jo White, who entered college for the spring semester last year, and who thus will be eligible for varsity competition on February 12. Besides everything else, KU positively leads the

world in keeping a little something for rainy days. Here is a potential star popping up at midseason."

1965-66: OUT-OF-BOUNDS

The 1965-66 Kansas team featured All-American Walt Wesley and veterans Al Lopes, Ron Franz and Del Lewis, but much of the excitement surrounded Jo Jo White, a 6-foot-3 guard who would join the varsity in the second half of the season. White had entered school in the middle of the season the year before, making him eligible for the second semester of the 1965-66 season. KU made the most of his arrival.

The Jayhawks trailed by one game in the conference standings when White joined the team, then won seven straight games to claim their first outright conference title in nine years.

KU advanced to the NCAA Regional at Lubbock, Texas, to face Southern Methodist in the first round. KU, led by Wesley's 23 points, won 76-70. Franz added 19, Lopes 11 and White 10 as the Jayhawks pulled away from a 46-46 halftime tie.

Walt Wesley, an All-American in 1966, is No. 13 on the KU scoring list with 1,315 points.

That set up the regional final against Texas Western (now Texas-El Paso). KU trailed 38-35 at the half, but White tied the game with 38 seconds to play in regulation, hitting his shot and the ensuing free throw to send the game to its first overtime at 69-69. The score was 71-71 when White let loose a 30-foot jumper that went in as the buzzer sounded to end the first overtime. But an official ruled that White's heel was on the out-of-bounds line, and the game went to a second overtime, where Texas Western won 81-80.

Texas Western went on to beat Kentucky for the NCAA title, providing Owens with what he would later call his "biggest disappointment."

According to a 1970 Wichita Eagle article, Owens used to stay after KU practices, making imaginary shots from the same spot as White's attempt:

> "'I've made that pivot of Jo Jo's hundreds of times … but I'm still not sure that his heel was actually touching the line,' Owens said. 'To the referee's credit, he called the play before the ball ever went through the basket. …'
>
> "'I still feel that if we had beaten Texas Western, we would have won the NCAA title.'"

WALT WESLEY Wesley led KU in scoring in 1965, averaging 23.5 points per game, and in 1966, averaging 20.7.

He was named All-Big Eight both years. He added All-America honors in 1966 and was drafted in the NBA's first round by Cincinnati. He played professionally until 1976, wrapping up his career with the Los Angeles Lakers.

35. In 1966-67, Vernon Vanoy became the first KU player to do this since the early 1950s. What was it?

1966-67: BACK-TO-BACK TRIPS TO THE DANCE

KU lost Wesley, Lopes and Lewis from the 1965-66 team but returned White, Franz and two top reserves, Rodger Bohnenstiehl and Bob Wilson. The Jayhawks also had a sophomore class that Owens called his best to that point. That class included 6-foot-8 bruiser Vernon Vanoy

As a junior, Walt Wesley scored 42 points against Loyola-Chicago – a performance tied for eighth on KU's all-time single-game scoring list.

and 6-7 Howard Arndt.

Bohnenstiehl led the Jayhawks in scoring with a 16.4 point average despite suffering several minor injuries, including two cuts to the head that required a total of 22 stitches, prompting one writer to note, "Bohnenstiehl leads the Big Eight in shooting and stitches."

The Jayhawks finished the conference season 13-1 for their second-straight conference title and earned the school's first back-to-back trips to the NCAA Tournament in 14 years.

Despite playing in Lawrence, the Jayhawks fell in the first round to Houston 66-53. White scored 18 points in the game and had 22 the next night as KU beat Louisville 70-68 in a regional consolation game.

The hype surrounding the start of the 1968-69 season concerned a battle between Oregon State, Kentucky and Kansas to be the first school to reach 1,000 victories. KU was 16 games away at the beginning of the season, but Kentucky was first to the mark.

1967-68: FALLING SHORT

With White and Bohnenstiehl back, KU's goal at the beginning of the 1967-68 season was to become the first Big Eight team to qualify for three straight NCAA Tournaments. It didn't happen.

A 19-7 overall record and a second-place finish in the Big Eight were only good enough for the school's first berth in the National Invitation Tournament.

Kansas had started the season with a non-conference schedule that Owens called "the toughest we've ever faced."

Before the Big Eight preseason tournament, KU faced a home-and-home series with defending Missouri Valley champion Louisville and single games against Utah State, Loyola-Chicago, Cincinnati, Texas A&M, St. Louis and Stanford. The Jayhawks went 6-2 in the stretch, losing only to Louisville and Loyola.

But losses to Kansas State and Nebraska late in the conference season left KU with a 10-4 Big Eight record.

Junior guard Phil Harmon lit up Temple for 21 points in KU's first-round NIT game in New York, leading KU to an 82-76 victory as Jo Jo added 19 points, Dave Nash 17 and Bohnenstiehl 15. Bohnenstiehl again scored 15 as KU beat Villanova 55-49 in the second round. Bohnenstiehl then scored 17 points and White 16 in the semifinal as KU beat St. Peter's 58-46.

The NIT final pitted KU against Dayton, and the game was tied at halftime, 25-25. But Dayton pulled away in the second half to win 61-48 in front of 19,000 at Madison Square Garden. Bohnenstiehl scored 12 points, bringing his tournament average to 14.7 a game.

Rodger Bohnenstiehl wore No. 35, the same Jayhawk jersey number worn by two future KU athletic directors : Monte Johnson and Bob Frederick.

OLYMPIC SUPERSTAR White had gained a great deal of

Kansas has produced 12 basketball Olympians, more than any other school.

1948: Gordon Carpenter

1952: Charles Hoag, Bill Hougland, John Keller, Dean Kelley, Bob Kenney, Bill Lienhard, Clyde Lovellette

1956: Bill Hougland

1960: Allen Kelley

1968: Jo Jo White

1980: Darnell Valentine

1988: Danny Manning

international experience by 1968, having played on the U.S. teams in the 1967 University Games in Tokyo and the 1967 Pan American Games. But nothing could compare with his appearance with the U.S. team at the 1968 Olympics in Mexico City.

White was the No. 2 scorer on that team, averaging 11.7 points over nine games, as the United States won its seventh straight Olympic gold medal.

In a Jan. 26, 1969, Topeka Capital-Journal article that ran before White's final KU game, he talked about his experience in Mexico City.

"My biggest thrill came in the Olympics," he said. "Just winning it made you feel so good because so many sportswriters had said we weren't a strong team."

TOUGH TO SAY GOODBYE Jo Jo White had only one semester of eligibility left heading into the 1968-69 season. He played his last game for the Jayhawks on Feb. 1, 1969, in Allen Fieldhouse and scored a career-high 30 points against Colorado in an 80-70 victory.

KU won 80 percent of its games with him in the lineup. He was an all-conference selection three times and a two-time All-American (1968, 1969).

White was something special from his first day at KU, Owens told the Topeka Capital-Journal in January 1969:

> "The first day he practiced was the first time I'd seen him play. It was obvious he had a lot of poise for a young man just stepping in. You couldn't help but notice his movement … how graceful he was."

White played 11 seasons in the NBA with Boston, Golden State and Kansas City, and his No. 10 jersey was retired by Boston. He later returned to Kansas as an assistant coach.

PUT THAT TRUMPET DOWN Bud Stallworth was discovered by the Jayhawks and Ted Owens by accident, Sports Illustrated reported in its March 1, 1971 issue: "Nobody at Kansas knew about him until he came from Alabama with a trumpet on his knee to a summer music camp. Jo Jo White, Kansas' superb backcourt man, saw him play pickup and alerted Owens."

1970-71: FINAL FOUR AGAIN

Owens began the 1970-71 season with a 12-man team that included nine returning lettermen and seven players who had started for the Jayhawks at some point. Led by

All-American Dave Robisch, Kansas streaked to a 25-1 regular-season record, the best in school history, and went undefeated in league play. The team joined the 1959 K-State team as the only ones to go through the eight-team league schedule unbeaten.

More important, KU advanced to the NCAA Final Four for the first time in seven years.

In regional play in Wichita, KU beat Houston 78-77 behind Robisch's 29 points and Stallworth's 25. KU beat Drake 73-71 in the final, as Robisch scored 27 points.

The victory sent KU to Houston for a matchup with five-time NCAA champion UCLA, ranked No. 1 in the nation at the time. Although KU and UCLA had the same 27-1 records heading into the game, KU had struggled, winning its last six games by a total of 13 points, two of them in overtime. Three days before the KU-UCLA game, Owens spoke about the matchup:

"I think every coach dreams about how to play UCLA. Every time I've seen them on television, I've

Dave Robisch was the Big Eight scoriing champion in 1970, averaging 26.6 points a game.

wondered how to play them."

But he didn't quite figure it out. KU never recovered from a seven-point halftime deficit and lost 68-60. Robisch scored 17 points and Stallworth and Pierre Russell added 12 each as KU's 21-game winning streak came to an end.

Robisch and Stallworth, already named All-Big Eight, were named to the NCAA All-Tournament team.

ROBISCH MOVES ON With 1,754 points, Robisch ended his career as KU's second all-time scorer, trailing only Clyde Lovellettte. Robisch now ranks fourth on the all-time list. He led the Big Eight in scoring in the 1969-70 season, averaging 26.6 points a game. Robisch, who was a letterman on the KU baseball team as a left-handed pitcher, also was courted by pro baseball scouts. But he chose pro basketball and was selected in the fifth round in 1971 by the ABA's Denver Rockets. He went on to play 13 seasons in the ABA and the NBA before retiring in 1984.

BUD PUTS ON A SHOW Ninth-ranked Missouri visited Allen Fieldhouse on Feb. 26, 1972, but the highly rated Tigers weren't the most distinguished guests at the game that day. Thirteen members of the 1952 championship team were in attendance as part of a 20th anniversary ceremony honoring their accomplishment. Before the game, Owens told the Kansan, "I don't know whether they will have any effect, but I know that if I were a player, having those great players there would be just added incentive to play well."

Bud Stallworth must have agreed. Stallworth scored 50 points as KU upset the Tigers 93-80. He was 19 of 38 from the field and 12 of 13 from the line and scored 24 of KU's first 30 points. Stallworth was the only Jayhawk in double figures that day and didn't reach the 50-point mark until he hit two free throws with seven seconds remaining.

Stallworth's mother was at the game, the first time she had seen her son play in Allen Fieldhouse. Afterward, Stallworth was fairly subdued about his accomplishment:

"Once you get started, it's hard to cool off."

Stallworth, who had been selected an Academic All-American in 1971, was a consensus All-American selection in 1972 and was named KU's Most Valuable Player. He was a first-round pick of the Seattle SuperSonics in 1972 and played five seasons in the NBA with Seattle and New Orleans.

Bud Stallworth, whose real first name was Isaac, lettered at KU from 1970 to 1972.

Bud Stallworth brings the ball upcourt against Western Kentucky in a Dec. 20, 1969, game in Lawrence. KU won 104-81.

1973-74: BOUNCING BACK

In one of the more dramatic turnarounds in college basketball history, the Jayhawks bounced back from an 8-18 record in 1972-73 to become one of the top teams in the nation. The Jayhawks, 23-7, battled all the way to the Final Four, becoming the first team in 23 years to come off a losing season and charge to the NCAA finals (Santa Clara in 1951 was the first).

The team's leader was all-conference selection Tom Kivisto, one of only two seniors. He was only the No. 6 scorer on the team, but Owens considered him the quarterback.

Balance was a key for the Jayhawks. The scoring mix of juniors Danny Knight (12.4 points a game), Roger Morningstar (12.3), Dale Greenlee (11.8) and Rick Suttle (11.3) and freshman Norm Cook (11.4) – the NCAA had declared freshmen eligible for varsity play in 1973 – provided the spark for KU. The season was the first in KU history in which five players scored more than 300

KU QUIZ

36. This KU graduate began a long broadcasting career as the Voice of the Jayhawks in the 1967-68 season. Who?

points and five players had averaged in double figures.

The key game in the conference race was on March 6 in Allen Fieldhouse. The championship boiled down to K-State vs. KU.

Kansas won the game 60-55 and the Big Eight title, sparking a midnight celebration by 7,000 students in front of Watson Library, the Alumni Magazine reported.

In the Midwest Regional in Tulsa, last-minute wins against Creighton and Oral Roberts University clinched a spot for the Jayhawks in the Final Four, set for Greensboro, N.C.

The Jayhawks lost their national semifinal game to Marquette 64-51. KU also dropped the third-place game to UCLA, 78-61. North Carolina State won the tournament.

"Certainly I'm disappointed and the players are disappointed we didn't play better," Owens said after losing both games. "We are a much better basketball team than we demonstrated. But at the same time, I'm

Tom Kivisto holds the KU single-game assist record. He had 18 against Nebraska on Dec. 29, 1973.

so darned proud of this team I can't even begin to explain it. In the 14 years I've been at KU, I can't think of a squad as dedicated and determined as this one."

1974-75: A FOUL ENDING

Six lettermen returned from the 1973-74 Final Four team, but the Jayhawks had to replace Kivisto.

KU was 17-7 overall and in a tie with Kansas State for the Big Eight lead at 9-3 when the Jayhawks traveled to Lincoln to meet Nebraska in the next-to-last league game. Nebraska was struggling in fourth place in the Big Eight, but Owens was concerned about the game, especially considering that the Cornhuskers would be playing their last game in their 8,000-seat Coliseum before moving to a new 15,000-seat arena.

Owens was right. KU struggled, committing eight turnovers in the first eight minutes of the game. The Jayhawks still trailed by five points with 48 seconds left in the game when things got really interesting.

KU's Rick Suttle was fouled and made the first free throw, but he missed the second intentionally. Sophomore Norm Cook rebounded and scored, cutting the lead to 67-65. On the inbounds play, the Jayhawks fouled Nebraska's Jerry Fort. He missed the free throw, and Suttle scored for KU with 13 second to go, sending the game to its first overtime. KU won in the second overtime 79-77.

Suttle finished with 29 points and 16 rebounds, and KU moved to 10-3, clinching at least a share of the Big Eight title because Kansas State had lost at Missouri the same night. With a win against Oklahoma three days later, KU clinched its second-straight Big Eight title and a berth in the NCAA Tournament.

The Jayhawks were sent to Tulsa to meet Notre Dame and All-American Adrian Dantley in the first round. The story of the game was at the free-throw line. KU collected 39 fouls to Notre Dame's 19, and the Irish made 35 of 50 from the line, accounting for nearly half of their points in their 77-71 win. Five KU players fouled out: Donnie Von Moore, Norm Cook, Clint Johnson, Dale Greenlee and Milt Gibson. Dantley led all scorers with 33 points, 15 of them coming at the line.

On the list of career disqualifications for fouling out of games, players during the Ted Owens era own the top five spots:

1. Ken Koenigs (1975-78) 32

2. Paul Mokeski (1976-79) 25

3. Darnell Valentine (1978-81) 23

4. Vernon Vanoy (1967-68) 22

5. Roger Brown (1969-71) 21

(Danny Manning also has 21.)

OOPS Kansas State traveled to Allen Fieldhouse on Feb. 12, 1977, for a game that was broadcast nationally on NBC. The 16,138 fans in attendance and those in televisionland were treated to a thriller. With 33 seconds

Ken Koenigs led the Jayhawks in free-throw percentage in 1975-76 (75.8 percent) and 1976-77 (84.7 percent).

Norm Cook is 10th on KU's career rebounds list with 624, an average of 7.5 a game. He also is a member of the Jayhawks' 1,000-point club...barely. He finished his career with 1,004 points.

remaining, KU co-captain Ken Koenigs hit two free throws to tie the game at 83. But Koenigs' reign as a hero was short-lived.

After K-State failed to inbound the ball in five seconds, KU took possession. Koenigs counted to three in his head while trying to inbound the ball (just as Owens had drilled his players to do) and when he couldn't, he called time out. But KU had already used its allotted four time-outs, and Koenigs was charged with a technical foul.

K-State's Curtis Redding hit the free throw for his 34th point. The Wildcats had the lead and the ball and scored once more to wrap up an 86-83 victory. Several days later, Big Eight supervisor of officials Bernie Saggau said there actually should have been a jump ball after the technical shot because of the "false double foul" rule – both teams had committed infractions back-to-back.

The score still would have been 84-83 in favor of K-

State at the jump ball, and KU players and coaches weren't about to say they should've or could've won. That's because KU had missed three wide-open layups in the late going and Owens had called time out to make a substitution that he later said was unnecessary.

"If there's anyone to blame," Owens said in the Kansan, "it's me for not having a time-out left."

DON'T BLAME THE COACH The heat on the KU coaches continued after the 1976-77 season was over, with KU finishing 18-10 overall and fourth in the conference.

But the KU players were quick to defend Owens and his staff, according to a wire story:

> "'I don't think they should take the blame for us losing 10 ball games,' said Ken Koenigs, a junior forward. 'Sure, we should have done better. But they didn't lose the games for us.'
>
> "John Douglas, all-conference guard, said he feels Owens and his staff have done a good job.
>
> "'He's the best coach in the Big Eight. He shouldn't be fired,' Douglas said."

TRADITION Owens put the history and tradition of KU basketball to good use on the recruiting trail, according to Sports Illustrated in Feb. 13, 1978:

"One of their gimmicks is a picture of Allen Field House atop Mount Oread, with the faces of Naismith, Allen and Owens gazing from the side of the hill like the Presidents on Mount Rushmore."

TRADITION? In that same Sports Illustrated article:

> "'People talk about the other coaches who have been here, but Owens is the only one I've heard of,' says freshman star Darnell Valentine. Old-time Kansas fans would have cringed had they heard Valentine and another freshman, Wilmore Fowler, try to recall the name of the man who went from Kansas to Kentucky to the Naismith Hall of Fame. 'Adolph Rump,' said Valentine. 'Rudolph Hupp,' said Fowler. As for Naismith, Guard John Douglas asked recently, 'Was he the dude who invented the ball?'"

John Douglas lettered in 1977 and '78 and was quick to defend Owens when the KU coach came under fire.

1977-78: BRUINS DO IT AGAIN

Back in 1971, Owens had said that every coach dreams of playing UCLA. Well, he got another shot at it in the 1977-78 season.

Wilmore Fowler teamed with Darnell Valentine to give the Jayhawks a deadly backcourt duo in 1978 and '79.

KU (led by freshman Darnell Valentine and senior Ken Koenigs, both All-Big Eight selections) had won its sixth Big Eight title under Owens. Although the Jayhawks had beaten K-State twice during the season, the Wildcats prevailed in the Big Eight Tourney, winning 87-76 in Kansas City.

KU still made the NCAA field but was sent to the West Regional in Eugene, Ore., to face UCLA in the first round. Once again, fouls were the Jayhawks' demise.

KU outscored UCLA 68-56 from the field, but UCLA was 27 of 39 from the free-throw line and KU only 8 of 17. UCLA won 83-76. The Jayhawks led 45-42 at half-time and still held on to the lead as late as 2:37 left in the game. But Valentine, Koenigs and Clint Johnson all fouled out, and UCLA pulled away. Junior center Paul Mokeski led the Jayhawks with 18 points and 12 rebounds.

OOPS II KU was 4-0 early in the 1978-79 season when the Jayhawks visited Kentucky on Dec. 9. KU was ranked fifth in the country, and Kentucky, the defending national champion, was No. 10.

Kansas led 35-28 at intermission but went into a four-corners offense in the second half when it ran into foul trouble. That allowed Kentucky to whittle away at the lead, and the score was 56-56 at the end of regulation.

The Jayhawks had pulled ahead by six points with 31 seconds left in the overtime. But they saw Kentucky hit two baskets and two free throws to tie it at 66 with three seconds remaining. After Kentucky's second free throw, Mac Stallcup and at least two other Jayhawks all called time out.

KU didn't have one.

Kyle Macy hit the free throw for Kentucky, and the Wildcats won 67-66.

"It was strictly instinct," Stallcup said in the Kansan.

It was a tough loss that partially set the tone for what became a frustrating season. Despite having Valentine, Mokeski, Wilmore Fowler and freshmen Tony Guy and David Magley, KU finished 18-11 overall and 8-6 in the Big Eight for a second-place tie.

TED LOSES IT Before a home game against Oklahoma on Feb. 10, 1979, KU was presented with the Big Eight Sportsmanship award. Owens then promptly showed just how sportsmanlike he could be.

KU superstar Darnell Valentine had stolen the ball and was racing the length of the court for a layup when

The conference held its first postseason Big Eight tourney after the 1976-77 season. K-State won the tournament title, beating Missouri 72-67 in overtime to earn the conference's NCAA berth. KU has won the postseason tournament four times: 1981, 1984, 1986 and 1992.

Paul Mokeski is fifth on KU's career blocked shots list with 136. He had seven against Fairleigh Dickinson in November 1978, which set a KU record, later tied twice by Danny Manning.

OU's Terry Stotts undercut him from behind, sending Valentine flying into the padded support for the goal.

Valentine was all right, but Owens lost his cool and rushed the Oklahoma bench. He was outraged because he believed that the KU guard had been the target of rough tactics in the league. A column in the Wichita Eagle gave this account of Owens' outburst:

The most popular T-shirt in Lawrence in 1977: a red shirt with white lettering with the message "Gong Owens" across the chest, a reference to television's "The Gong Show."

> "The Kansas coach pushed his way into the Oklahoma bench area and was seen swinging his arm at OU coach Dave Bliss. There was some shoving before Sooners' star John McCullough pulled Owens away. One of the officials, John Dabrow of Wichita, finally escorted Owens back toward the KU bench. Owens was not dealt a technical foul. …

Bliss called Owens' actions "ungentlemanly." An Oklahoma sportscaster called Owens "a bush-leaguer."

KU won the game 74-62, with Valentine scoring 19 points.

ALL YOU NEED IS LOVE KU lost to Kansas State 61-52 in

Lawrence on Jan. 19, 1980, in a game that featured loud booing from the fans in Allen Fieldhouse – mostly directed at the Jayhawks.

But KU assistant coach Bob Hill had it all figured out. After a practice and just a couple of days before Kansas beat Missouri, Hill said: "What this team lacks is love. There's no love.

"And you can't teach love. You have to recruit it."

TED-BASHING ON THE ROAD Even road teams, such as Missouri, got in on the Owens-bashing, according to a wire story on Feb. 14, 1980:

"There were derogatory signs draped over the balcony of the Hearnes Center and even a flier being passed out urging Kansas Athletic Director Bob Marcum, "Don't Fire Ted." ("Is it right for one school to deprive the other seven schools in the conference of a valuable asset to their programs?" said the handout.)"

A wood floor was installed before the 1979-80 season to replace a synthetic surface that had been used since 1974-75. It didn't help the team much. KU went 15-14 overall and 7-7 in the Big Eight for a third-place finish.

SOONER BE A JAYHAWK Oklahoma went after one of its native sons and former players in 1980 to fill its coaching vacancy. The word was that the job was Owens' for the taking. And many thought he would head south to Norman.

The heat had been on Owens at Kansas, and rumors persisted that he would be fired. According to the Wichita Eagle on March 19, 1980, Owens had practically demanded that KU officials issue a statement of support two weeks earlier. He said that the rumors were hurting his recruiting efforts.

His ties to Oklahoma basketball were strong. He was an all-conference player at OU from 1949 to 1951.

But Owens chose to stick with KU, and the Sooner job went to Billy Tubbs.

"I have developed a deep love for KU over the last 20 years, and I look forward to the challenge of next year returning our team to the level of excellence that it has enjoyed," Owens said.

1980-81: ONE MORE TIME

As had been his habit at KU, Owens again found a way to win with the Jayhawks. He rebounded from three mediocre seasons to take KU to the NCAA Tournament and buy himself some more time with the Jayhawk faithful.

The Jayhawks returned nine lettermen for 1980-81, including All-America guard Darnell Valentine, Tony

Guy, Booty Neal, John Crawford, Dave Magley, Art Housey and Kelly Knight.

The first half of the season brought only two losses (Michigan and Kentucky) as the Jayhawks rolled to a 14-2 mark before falling to Kansas State 54-43 in Manhattan on Jan. 28. KU then went into a slump, losing four of five games, including a triple-overtime loss to Oklahoma State in Stillwater. Even with a strong finish, the Jayhawks did no better than tie for second in the Big Eight at 9-5. KU still made the NCAA field and was sent to the sub-regional in Wichita, giving plenty of Jayhawk fans the chance to see their team in postseason.

Valentine, who had been a standout at Wichita's Heights High School, was back in front of his hometown fans and led KU with 15 points as the Jayhawks beat Mississippi 69-66 in the first round. Tony Guy was the star of the final game in Wichita, scoring 36 points and collecting five rebounds as KU beat Arizona State 88-71 to advance to the Midwest Regional in New Orleans.

Dave Magley (35) was co-captain of the 1981-82 KU team and led the Jayhawks in scoring that season, averaging 17.3 points a game.

KU's first game in New Orleans was a matchup that Wichita State fans had waited 26 years for. The feeling in Wichita was that the Jayhawks thought they were too good to play the Shockers. In a game dubbed the "Battle of New Orleans," Wichita State exacted its revenge, defeating KU 66-65.

The WSU fans in New Orleans had placed ads in the Louisiana papers asking LSU fans to cheer for them. It worked, and the Shockers were backed by a loud contingent in the Superdome.

With six seconds remaining, WSU reserve guard Mike Jones hit a 30-foot jump shot that put the Shockers up by one. KU called time out, and the clock was stopped with two seconds remaining and the Jayhawks in possession of the ball under the WSU goal.

Booty Neal was set to throw the ball inbounds when Valentine tried to draw a foul on the inbounds play, but it wasn't called. KU called time out again and set up a full-court pass that was too long. WSU had the victory.

KU guard Darnell Valentine signed autographs for some young fans on Valentine's Day in 1978.

"I think about 30,000 people knew it was a foul, but three didn't call it," Owens said after the game. "I don't like to be unkind, but it was obviously a flagrant foul."

DARNELL VALENTINE The Wichita State game was Valentine's last as a Jayhawk and had both its high and low points. He led KU with 21 points but also missed a layup and the front end of a one-and-one during the last minute of the game. He finished his career as the KU assist leader with 609, was an All-American in 1981, was a three-time Academic All-American and was All-Big Eight in 1978, '79, '80 and '81, the first four-time selection. He finished third on KU's career scoring list with 1,821 points and was a member of the 1980 Olympic team that boycotted the games in Moscow. Picked in the first round by the Portland Trailblazers, he played in the NBA until 1989.

37. Three men served as athletic director during six months in 1983. Who where they?

300 WINS AND STILL A TOUGH CROWD Sixteen years after taking the head coaching position at KU, Owens won the 300th game of his career, 81-67 against Pepperdine on Dec. 1, 1980.

Despite joining some elite coaching company, times were still rough for Owens.

When he was honored for his accomplishment before the next game, he was greeted by a mix of applause and boos from the Allen Fieldhouse crowd.

SMILING AT DISASTER Heading into the 1982-83 season, KU was coming off of a 13-14 finish, its first losing record in nine years, and a seventh-place finish in the Big Eight, its lowest in 20 years.

But things were looking up for the Jayhawks. Carl Henry was eligible after sitting out a year following his transfer from Oklahoma City University. And a strong recruiting class, which included Ron Kellogg, Calvin Thompson, Kerry Boagni and Jeff Guiot, would help.

Owens said he saw better days ahead in 1982-83:

"This may sound a little crazy," he said, "but I feel better about the program than I have in a long time. I'm optimistic about the future. I don't feel down at all."

THE END FOR TED It was all wishful thinking. The Jayhawks ended that season tied for last place in the conference at 4-10 and 13-16 overall. The back-to-back losing seasons and an average of 5,500 empty seats for every game meant the end for Owens. He was fired March 21, 1983, after 19 years as head coach, becoming the only basketball coach ever fired by the university.

Monte Johnson, KU's new athletic director, said the move was made to remove the inconsistency that had plagued the program dating to about 1970 and to return

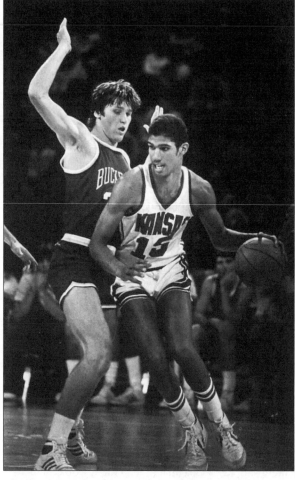

Kerry Boagni, recruited to KU by Ted Owens, left midway through the 1983-84 season under Owens' successor, Larry Brown.

it to being a national power.

Owens did not speak publicly about his firing until that year's basketball banquet. It became an emotional good-bye, the Wichita Eagle reported on April 6, 1983:

> "'I won't say I don't have anger and bitterness. It comes and goes. I am so disappointed I won't have a chance to work with this bunch next year.'
>
> "Then the tears began to come in his eyes.
>
> "'Only history will determine what kind of career we had here,' he said. 'I don't know who will be the new coach here, but no one could love this place more than me.'
>
> "His voice broke. He reached for his napkin and wiped his eyes. He had said his farewell."

After he was fired at KU, Ted Owens coached two years at Oral Roberts University, one season in a professional league in California and one in a professional league in Israel before becoming the chief fundraiser and head basketball coach at Metro Christian Academy in Tulsa, Okla., where he's pictured above in a 1991 photo.

Larry Brown

Years Coached At KU: 1983-1988
KU Record: 135-44, .754 winning percentage

Larry Brown spent five years in Kansas. The stint was the shortest for a Jayhawk coach; but for Brown, it must have seemed like an eternity.

He had a reputation in coaching for not sticking around, but he spent more time in Lawrence than he had in any other place. His career with the Jayhawks culminated in a national championship in 1988.

Brown graduated from North Carolina in 1963, where he was an honorable-mention All-America guard under former Jayhawk Dean Smith. Brown played on the 1964 Olympic basketball team, played and coached at the professional level and took UCLA to the national finals in 1980.

He left KU after he was offered a multimillion dollar contract to coach the San Antonio Spurs of the NBA. During his tenure, Kansas appeared in five straight NCAA Tournaments, won the 1985-86 Big Eight championship, won two Big Eight Tournament titles, made two trips to the Final Four and won its first national championship since 1952. He was Big Eight Coach of the Year in 1986, and he coached Danny Manning, consensus Player of the Year in 1988 and an All-American at Kansas.

Since leaving the Jayhawks, Brown has coached the Spurs, the Clippers and the Pacers of the NBA.

Jayhawk fans never questioned Brown's credentials when he came to Lawrence, only how long he would stay.

1983-84: BROWN TAKES KU BACK TO THE BIG DANCE

Despite a seventh-place conference finish in 1982-83, Ted Owens did not exactly leave the cupboard bare for Larry Brown. The Jayhawks were led by the experience of Carl Henry, Kelly Knight and Brian Martin. Greg Dreiling was eligible to play, and sophomores Ron Kellogg and Calvin Thompson returned. Brown used that combination to lead KU to a 22-10 overall record and a 9-5 mark in the conference as KU won the postseason Big Eight Tournament and advanced to the second round of the NCAA Tournament.

AMAZING COINCIDENCE On Sept. 20, 1983, Brown announced that he had hired Ed Manning as an assistant coach to replace Jo Jo White, who he had fired during the summer.

"He's a great communicator," Brown said of Manning in a Kansan story. "He does relate to the kids well, and I'm just happy that he's going to be with us.

"The most important thing is that I feel comfortable with him."

Of course, it's easy to feel comfortable with a guy who has a 6-10 future All-American as a son. Two days later, Danny Manning announced that he would attend KU in the fall. Manning had narrowed his choices to North Carolina and KU, and even Dean Smith could see what

Larry Brown and his staff had some interesting superstitions. The coaches all ran and didn't shave on game days, and they never wore paisley ties. And if the Jayhawks lost a game, the coaches never wore the same clothes to a game again.

Danny and Ed Manning, shown here with the Wooden Award in 1988, were a package deal for KU.

KU QUIZ

38. Why did Brown come to hate trips to the Hilton Coliseum in Ames, Iowa?

was coming.

"Coach Smith sat down and talked with me," Manning told the Kansan. "He told me that if I didn't go to North Carolina, he wanted me to go to KU."

Manning wanted to get the announcement out of the way before his senior season, which he played at Lawrence High School after transferring from Greensboro, N.C. Danny said he wanted to stay close to home, and with Dad's new job, home was Lawrence.

A FAMILIAR FOE Greg Dreiling found himself just a tad nervous when the Wichita State Shockers, his former team, visited Allen Fieldhouse on Feb. 5, 1984. "I was about ready to throw up," Dreiling told the Kansan. But he relaxed during the game, despite the jeers of WSU fans in the crowd, and scored 14 points to help KU to a 79-69 victory.

A CLASH WITH ACADEMIA A furor erupted on campus in

It was Ted Owens who convinced Greg Dreiling to transfer to KU from Wichita State. But the 7-footer had to sit out Owens' final season under NCAA rules.

February 1984 when the Kansan reported that Brown
had accompanied Cedric Hunter to visit a history
professor, David Katzman. Katzman said Brown tried to
get him to raise Hunter's failing grade in his American
History class. Brown said he only went along for moral
support and out of a responsibility to his player. Hunter
did fail the course and was ruled academically ineligible
for the spring semester.

SOONERS STRUT Things turned downright ugly when
Wayman Tisdale and the eighth-ranked Oklahoma
Sooners traveled to Lawrence on Feb. 22, 1984. Calvin
Thompson capped a furious second-half rally by hitting a
30-foot shot at the buzzer to send the game to overtime.
But the Sooners romped in the extra period, outscoring
KU 18-8 and winning 92-82 to clinch the Big Eight title.
The KU crowd showered the court with debris when OU
coach Billy Tubbs called time out late in the overtime to
let his players gloat.

KU QUIZ

Brown went to the microphone to plead with the
crowd: "Let's show a little sportsmanship. They deserve
the game. Let's cut it out."

But things only got worse. When the game ended, the
Sooners cut down the nets to celebrate their crown, and
the fans threw more debris. On his way off the floor,
OU's David Johnson and three KU fans got into a fist-
fight that ended quickly.

39. Why was Calvin
Thompson's nick-
name "Pony?"

"They were throwing things at us, so we said after the
game that we were going to show 'em who's number
one," Sooner guard Jan Pannell said in the Kansan. "If
we ever get the opportunity to stick our hand up or stick
our finger up and say 'We're number one,' we are going
to do it."

PERFECT ENOUGH The Jayhawks visited Manhattan, Kan.,
on Feb. 25, 1984, looking to clinch second place in the
Big Eight, which would be their highest finish since
1978. But it took a miracle to pull it off in front of 11,220
fans at Ahearn Fieldhouse.

KU had gone to a stall game with three minutes
remaining to try to pull K-State out of a sagging zone
that had bothered the Jayhawks all night. The Wildcats,
led by Tom Alfaro's 23 points, had led by as many as five
points late.

But with the score tied 61-61 and time running out,
KU's Mark Turgeon passed the ball to Carl Henry, who
was 12 feet down the baseline, behind the basket, with
K-State's Eddie Elder in his face. Henry, who said

Carl Henry played two years with the NBA's Kings, the first season in Kansas City and the second after they moved to Sacramento.

afterward that he couldn't even see the basket from that angle, let loose a shot that went through with three seconds remaining, and KU won 63-61.

It wasn't the shot Brown wanted KU to take: "I don't think any coach designs a perfect shot," Brown said. "But the right guy made the right pass to the right player … and it went in.

"That's perfect enough."

BIG EIGHT TOURNEY TITLE After defeating Oklahoma State in Lawrence in the first round of the Big Eight Tourney (the top four seeds played at home sites in the first round from 1977 to 1985), KU met Kansas State in the semifinals at Kemper Arena in Kansas City, Mo., on March 9. The Jayhawks "held" K-State's Tommy Alfaro to 18 points, and Ron Kellogg was the defensive hero for a change, taking care of Alfaro when KU put on a box-and-one defense in the second half. Carl Henry and Calvin Thompson led KU's offense with 16 points each, and Greg Dreiling added 14 to help give KU a 70-59 victory and set up a rematch with Oklahoma in the tourney final.

Kellogg resumed his more accustomed role as an offensive standout against the Sooners when he hit a 15-foot jumper with 40 seconds remaining to give KU a 79-78 win over OU in the final. The win gave KU the Big Eight's automatic berth in the NCAA Tournament, although the Jayhawks, with 20 wins, were generally expected to receive an at-large bid. Carl Henry scored 30 points as KU held All-American Wayman Tisdale to 17 points, 10 below his average.

RIDING THE MOMENTUM The Jayhawks finally believed in themselves after the OU win, Brown said, and he was hoping they would run with that confidence in the NCAA Tournament. KU was a No. 5 seed in the Midwest Regional in Lincoln, Neb.

Ron Kellogg played on the U.S. team at the World University Games in 1985.

The Jayhawks met Alcorn State in their first-round game, a contest in which KU trailed for 38 minutes and 38 seconds. At that point, Kellogg followed his own missed shot to put KU ahead 55-54. But Aaron Brandon, who led Alcorn State with 18 points, hit a long jumper with just under a minute to go to put the Jayhawks back in a 56-55 hole. KU worked for a good last shot, and Kellogg tried a baseline jumper that missed. But Henry's shot off the miss with 12 seconds left put KU ahead 57-56.

Alcorn State had three shots in the last nine seconds,

but two missed and Kelly Knight blocked what seemed like an easy layup by Alcorn State's Davie Claybon at the buzzer, giving KU the win and a second-round date with Wake Forest.

DEMON DEACONS KU ran into a rugged 19th-ranked Wake Forest team, and the inside game of Anthony Teachey and Kenny Green was too much for the Jayhawks as they fell 69-59. Teachey dominated the boards, grabbing 15 rebounds as the Demon Deacons outrebounded KU 34-17. And Green scored most of his 20 points inside. Four KU players hit double figures: Knight with 12 points, Thompson with 11, Dreiling and Henry each with 10.

HE STAYED FOR DINNER Brown used the team's annual basketball banquet after the 1983-84 season to take a few jabs at those who said he wouldn't stay long:

"I haven't been to one of these banquets in a while," Brown said. "I guess I haven't stayed around long enough.

"I told my wife that we've stayed here four seasons – winter, summer, spring and fall."

Kelly Knight is the brother of the late Danny Knight, a member of KU's 1974 Final Four team.

1984-85: YOUNG GUNS

KU began the 1984-85 season with nine freshmen on the 15-man varsity squad, with Tad Boyle as the only senior. But Ron Kellogg, Calvin Thompson, Cedric Hunter and Mark Turgeon were back, and among those nine new faces was future All-American Danny Manning. The Jayhawks rolled to a 13-2 start, losing only to Alabama-Birmingham at the Great Alaska Shootout and to Kentucky by three points in late December.

The Jayhawks went on to a 26-8 overall record and an 11-3 mark that was good for another second-place finish in the Big Eight. KU lost in the second round of the NCAA Tournament to Auburn.

AGONY IN ANN ARBOR KU was 15-3 headed into a nationally televised game at Michigan on Jan. 27, 1985. But the Jayhawks should have stayed home in Lawrence. KU lost 96-77 in one of the most lopsided losses since Brown had arrived.

Near the end of the season, Brown had still not forgotten his trip to Ann Arbor or the way the Jayhawks played there.

"Michigan was ugly," he said.

Tad Boyle finished his career with 256 assists, 11th on KU's all-time list.

THOSE PESKY CYCLONES By Feb. 16, 1985, the Jayhawks had climbed to a No. 10 ranking in the AP poll when they traveled to Ames, Iowa. On a last-second, acrobatic shot, Iowa State's Jeff Hornacek beat the Jayhawks 72-70.

On March 9, after KU had defeated Nebraska in a first-round Big Eight Tournament game, the Cyclones once again rained on KU's parade. The Jayhawks were riding a five-game winning streak and were back to No. 10 in the national polls when ISU trounced them 75-59 in the second round. Hornacek scored 12 of his 16 points in the first half, and long-range shooter Barry Stevens finished with 25.

After the tournament loss to ISU, certain that his Jayhawks had severely damaged their seeding in the NCAA bracket, Brown asked only half jokingly: "Are you allowed to turn down a bid to the tournament?"

SLOW-MOTION BASKETBALL Most conferences across the nation had used the 45-second clock during the 1984-85 season. But it was not in use at the NCAA Tournament, and KU's first-round opponent made the most of that fact.

KU met an Ohio team coached by Danny Nee on March 14 in the Midwest sub-regional at South Bend, Ind. KU won 49-38 in what The Wichita Eagle described as "probably the first blowout in modern history in which the winning team scored a total of 49 points."

Nee said his strategy was simple:

"Our game plan was to make the 40-minute game a 25-minute game. That's just our style. ... We were familiar with holding the ball a little."

Freshman Danny Manning, nervous in his NCAA debut, came alive in the second half. In one four-minute stretch, he made a dazzling save and tossed the ball inbounds to Calvin Thompson for a 15-footer, fed Ron Kellogg for a short jumper, scored twice from the lane and grabbed three rebounds as KU took control of the game.

WINNING FOR SONNY KU met a team on a mission in its second-round game at South Bend: Sonny Smith's Auburn. The 11th-seeded Tigers, who had upset sixth-seeded Purdue 59-58 to advance, knew each game could be the last for Smith, who had resigned as their coach effective at the end of the season. They desperately wanted to beat KU and advance to the regional semifinals in Birmingham, Ala., to play in front of their home-state fans.

They did, upending KU 66-64. Dreiling and Manning got into foul trouble in the first half, and freshman Chris Piper got his first taste of NCAA action, playing 20 solid minutes before the game was over.

KU had struggled to a 52-50 lead when Auburn's Chuck Person and Frank Ford combined to move the Tigers ahead by seven. Ford scored 23 points, and Person finished with 21.

Despite three controversial intentional fouls called on KU late, Calvin Thompson pulled the Jayhawks back within 66-64. KU then had a chance to tie the game on a 15-footer by Manning at the buzzer that barely missed.

"This game got away from us," Kellogg said. "It hurt most that the season ended on a bad note."

1985-86: DALLAS-BOUND

All of the ingredients seemed to be there for the 1985-86 season. Calvin Thompson, Ron Kellogg and Greg Dreiling returned as seniors, and Danny Manning and Cedric Hunter were back with even more NCAA experience, in addition to reserves Chris Piper and Mark Turgeon.

And the combination worked. All five starters – Dreiling, Thompson, Manning, Kellogg and Hunter – started every game during the regular season as the team

KU QUIZ

40. Which two teams did KU beat while wearing red during the 1985-86 season?

Calvin Thompson dunks on Duke's Danny Ferry in the championship game of the Big Apple NIT, which kicked off the 1985-86 season. The teams would next meet in Dallas at the Final Four.

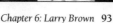

rolled to a 28-3 overall record and a Big Eight title with a 13-1 mark. KU then won the Big Eight Tournament and advanced to the Final Four, where the Jayhawks fell to Duke 71-67. They finished the season 35-4, the most wins for a KU team in one season.

PREVIEW OF THINGS TO COME KU beat Pepperdine and Washington to open the season with wins in the first two rounds of the Big Apple NIT preseason tournament, earning a trip to New York for the semifinals. Once there, the No. 5 Jayhawks beat No. 9 Louisville 83-78 as Calvin Thompson scored 25 points. Next up was Duke, and Mark Alarie and David Henderson combined for 51 points as the No. 6 Blue Devils won 92-86 to take the NIT title. Duke was 22 of 25 from the free-throw line, compared with KU's 6 of 9.

PRACTICE MAKES PERFECT KU recorded its 1,300th win on Dec. 3, 1985, but Brown was unimpressed with the milestone victory. After a sluggish home performance in which Kansas committed 20 turnovers and made only 12 of 23 free throws in beating Southern Illinois-Edwardsville 86-71, Brown sent the team back on the floor for a 45-minute postgame practice.

JIMMY V, THE PROPHET After seeing his North Carolina State team crushed at home 71-56 by the Jayhawks, Coach Jim Valvano predicted big things for KU:
"Kansas will be in the Final Four," he said.

MR. SATURDAY Ron Kellogg hit 9 of 11 long-range bombs in the second half against N. C. State on his way to 23 points. It was one of several stunning performances for Kellogg that season during Saturday-afternoon games on national television. Fred Mann, a columnist for the Wichita Eagle, said Kellogg's "idea of shot selection was waiting until he found a spot in the same time zone." The long bombs (worth only two points at the time, remember) drove Brown crazy, but Kellogg said he had figured his coach out: "If I miss it from long range, he says it's a bad shot. If I make it, it's a good shot."

COULDN'T WE PLAY A THIRD TIME? Kansas met eventual champion Louisville twice during the regular season, winning both games. On Nov. 29, the Jayhawks defeated the Cardinals in the semifinals of the Big Apple NIT, and on Jan. 25, KU won 71-69 in Lawrence.
    In the second game, Greg Dreiling hit two free throws

with a little more than a minute remaining to provide the final margin as KU won its 28th straight game at Allen Fieldhouse, tying the record set from 1969 to 1972.

HELLO, MEMPHIS Andre Turner, Memphis State's standout point guard, had a score to settle with the fifth-ranked Jayhawks when they visited Memphis on Jan. 4, 1986. He had missed the game between the two teams in Lawrence the season before because of his father's death. KU had won that game by four points. But in Memphis, Turner had nine assists, seven steals and scored 16 of his 20 points in the second half to bring the Tigers back from an 11-point deficit to an 83-80 overtime win.

Danny Manning mysteriously shrunk during his college career. Media guides for his first three seasons listed him at 6-11. But he was listed at 6-10 in his senior season. He is listed as 6-10 in NBA guides.

Ron Kellogg looks to pass against Iowa State in the Big Eight Tournament championship game on March 9, 1986.

Fans were asked to pick their all-time Kansas team during balloting in the 1985-86 season. The team:
Clyde Lovellette 1950-52
Wilt Chamberlain 1957-58
Jo Jo White 1966-69
Darnell Valentine 1978-81
Danny Manning 1985-88

A TOUCH OF REVENGE When KU traveled to Norman on Feb. 24, 1986, the Jayhawks found a way to get back at the Oklahoma Sooners for cutting down the KU nets the year before. The Jayhawks won OU 87-80, ending the Sooners' 48-game home winning streak in the Lloyd Noble Center. After the game, Brown said, "Winning here was as good a road victory as I've ever been involved with."

LEAVING IN STYLE When KU won its final home game on March 1, 1986, against Iowa State, the Jayhawks did a little celebrating. They had clinched KU's first Big Eight title since 1978 the week before, and Brown had warned his team to leave the nets intact because the Jayhawks had higher goals to reach. But when seniors Ron Kellogg, Calvin Thompson and Greg Dreiling arrived at the fieldhouse in tuxedos, fans could tell it might be a special day. (Dreiling had to go all the way to Salina, Kan., to find a tux that was big enough.) "We came here in style," Kellogg said, "and we wanted to go out in style."

KU avenged its earlier loss in Ames by beating Iowa State 90-70, and the seniors decided to claim the nets. Dreiling and Thompson hoisted Kellogg up to sit astride the rim, and he whacked away at the cords with dull scissors.

"I thought for sure we were going to lose a left-handed, 6-5 forward," Brown said. "We're going to have to learn how to do a better job of cutting down nets."

NO GOING-AWAY PRESENT KU met Kansas State in the first round of the Big Eight Tournament for what would prove to be Jack Hartman's final game as K-State's head coach. KU won 74-51. Dreiling had 19 points and Manning added 16 to send KU to the semifinal for a third meeting with Oklahoma.

KU QUIZ

41. What did the four coaches at the 1986 Midwest Regional have in common?

DREAMING OF DALLAS KU fans had long been talking about the Jayhawks going to the Final Four, and after KU beat K-State to open the Big Eight Tournament, even Brown gave in:

"I want the players to think about Dallas," he said in a Wichita Eagle story. "The way they've conducted themselves and how hard they've tried, I don't want them thinking of anything but the opportunity of going to Dallas. I'll be disappointed if we don't get there. We are playing so well right now."

CLOSE CALLS The Jayhawks beat the Sooners 72-70 when Danny Manning hit two free throws with six seconds remaining. But the Iowa State-KU game for the tournament title was even closer.

With KU leading 73-71, Iowa State's Jeff Hornacek picked off a KU pass and drove the length of the court. He dished off to Sam Hill, who slipped past Greg Dreiling. Two whistles were heard, one for traveling on Hill and one for a foul on Dreiling. The buzzer had already sounded and the officials decided since the

Danny Manning's accomplishments:

Consensus Player of the Year in 1988.

All-American in 1987 and 1988.

Three-time Big Eight Player of the Year

Big Eight's second-leading career rebounder and KU's all-time leader with 1,187.

All-time leading scorer at KU and in the Big Eight with 2,951 points.

Seventh-leading scorer in NCAA history.

Leading shot blocker in KU history.

Owner of NCAA record for career games played (147), started (146) and double-figure scoring games (132).

traveling infraction happened first, the foul didn't count. KU had the Big Eight Tournament title and a No. l seed in the Midwest Regional of the NCAA Tournament in Dayton, Ohio.

EASY DAYS IN DAYTON The Jayhawks coasted past North Carolina A&T 71-46 in the first round. Four Jayhawks scored in double figures as KU moved to 32-3: Manning with 15 points, Thompson 14, Dreiling 12 and Marshall 10. Ron Kellogg sat out the game with a strained foot.

In the second-round game against Temple, KU held the Owls to a season-low 43 points in winning 65-43. Dreiling was hampered by foul trouble. But Manning, Thompson and Kellogg each had 14 points as KU went on to the Midwest Regional in Kansas City's Kemper Arena, 38 miles from Lawrence.

ELEVEN EXTRA SECONDS KU's 1986 regional semifinal vic-

Mark Turgeon finished his KU career with 437 assists, fifth on KU's all-time list.

tory over Michigan State will always be remembered for the 11 seconds that the clock failed to tick off late in regulation. Many argue that the mistake cost the Spartans the game, but that might be stretching things a bit.

With 2:20 left in the game, Michigan State led by two points and the timer could not get the clock started as the Spartans brought the ball upcourt. MSU coach Jud Heathcote left the coach's box to complain to officials, and Brown argued that Heathcote should get a technical for leaving the box. During the haggling, Brown's ever-present, rolled-up program caught the referee's whistle. A technical was assessed on Brown, and the Spartans made both free throws, then added a basket to lead 80-74 with 1:08 to play. Michigan State didn't score again in regulation, and when Archie Marshall tipped in a Calvin Thompson miss with nine seconds left, the game was headed to overtime.

Danny Manning and Ron Kellogg had fouled out, and Thompson took control in overtime, scoring eight of his 26 points as KU won 96-86. MSU argued that Marshall's tip with nine seconds remaining would not have come in time if the clock had been running earlier. But Brown was also quick to point out that he would not have received a technical, which gave the Spartans two easy points, if the argument about the clock had not happened.

Danny Manning and Larry Brown often found themselves the subject of media attention as KU made its drive to the Final Four in 1986.

THERE'S NO PLACE LIKE HOME Kansas earned its first trip to the Final Four in 12 years by beating North Carolina

Larry Brown made the final snip to claim the nets in Kansas City after KU beat North Carolina State to advance to the 1986 Final Four.

State 75-67 in the regional final at their other home court, Kemper Arena. KU trailed 57-52 in the second half when Danny Manning went on a tear, scoring 10 straight points. Then Greg Dreiling made nine in a row and KU led 71-63 with less than a minute to play.

"There were 17,000 people chanting 'Rock Chalk Jayhawks!'" N.C. State coach Jimmy Valvano said. "I don't know what the hell that means."

SEEING RED Larry Brown broke out the red uniforms for the 1985-86 season, hoping that they might bring KU good luck. The Jayhawks had worn red in 1952 while winning the national championship and in 1957 when they finished second.

Heading into Dallas, Brown's Jayhawks were 2-0 when wearing red. Perhaps Brown should have stuck with the blue uniforms. Heading into the 1986 Final Four, blue had been worn by more NCAA champions than any other color.

DALLAS NIGHTMARE KU's shot at a national title ended on March 29 at Dallas' Reunion Arena when KU lost to Duke 71-67 in what was undoubtedly the most frustrating game of Danny Manning's college career. He scored only four points, and his two baskets came 34 minutes and 17 seconds apart. Manning and Dreiling got into early foul trouble, and Cedric Hunter joined them on the bench late in the game after all three had fouled out. Top reserve Archie Marshall also was lost with eight minutes to go in the game when he injured his knee.

Despite all that, KU was still in the game. With the score tied 67-67, Duke's Mark Alarie clanked a shot off the rim and Duke's Danny Ferry squeezed between two KU players to grab the rebound and lay it in for a 69-67 lead with 22 seconds remaining. Eleven seconds later, Kellogg drove the baseline and ran into Ferry. A charge was called on Kellogg, but Ferry missed the free throw, and KU still had a chance. With four seconds remaining, Kellogg launched a 20-footer that banged off the front of the rim. Duke's Tommy Amaker was fouled on the rebound and sank both shots for the final margin.

Duke's Johnny Dawkins had 24 points, and Kellogg led the Jayhawks with 22. But KU reserves Mark Turgeon, Archie Marshall and Chris Piper had come up big for the Jayhawks to keep them in the game. Marshall had 13 points when he went down.

Turgeon was the only KU player seen crying in the locker room after the game.

The Jayhawks had agreed to get flat-top haircuts if they advanced to the Final Four. The players followed through, but Brown backed out.
"Coach agreed to do it," Greg Dreiling said. "But I guess he figured he already had too much space up there on top."

"I've been a KU fan all my life," he said in the Wichita Eagle. "I guess I took it like a fan would."

1986-87: SWEET SIXTEEN

Despite the loss of Dreiling, Kellogg and Thompson from 1985-86, KU's Final Four appearance had produced high expectations for the Jayhawks. With Manning and Hunter returning as starters and with one of the top recruiting classes in the country, KU opened the season ranked eighth nationally. Highly touted freshmen Kevin Pritchard and Mark Randall joined the Jayhawks as Brown began his first season with players recruited entirely by his staff. The Jayhawks went 25-11 overall and 9-5 in the Big Eight to tie for second in the conference. Their season ended with a regional semifinal loss to Georgetown.

AT ARMS' LENGTH Cedric Hunter proved to be an amazing defender for Larry Brown, mostly because of his wingspan. Listed at 6 feet, Hunter was actually about 5-10. His arms, however, are 37 inches long, equal to those of a man about 6-7 or 6-8. Duke's Johnny Dawkins, one of Hunter's toughest defensive assignments in his career, said of Hunter: "He's the best defensive guard. ... He's so quick. And what arms. They stretch out forever."

THREE-POINT PAINT JOB KU and every other Division I school added a freshly painted line to their courts for the 1986-87 season, a 3-point arc 19 feet, 9 inches from the basket. Ron Kellogg and Calvin Thompson, long-range specialists who had graduated the year before, would have made good use of it, Brown said, sounding sad before the start of the 1986-87 season: "That line came in a little too late."

LARRY GIGGLES? Senior guard Mark Turgeon missed practice at the start of the 1986-87 season because of a knee injury, and freshman Kevin Pritchard was tabbed to replace him in an exhibition game in mid-November. Pritchard sounded plenty mature when he assessed his new role on the team: "Life is full of challenges, and this is one of them." But Larry Brown seemed to have trouble keeping a straight face: "I giggle every time I think about him. He's going to be great."

SHOCKED BY THE SHOCKERS On Jan. 6, 1987, KU experienced a rare upset from state rival Wichita State at

Levitt Arena in Wichita.

The Shockers, led by Henry Carr, slowed down the game, frustrating the Jayhawks and their superstar, Danny Manning.

Manning was held to 12 points, and the Shockers walked away 54-49 victors.

"We had been struggling as a team before that, and we really bottomed out against Wichita State," Mark Turgeon said later. Turgeon had five fouls and no points in the game. "I didn't do anything except foul in that game. It was a long next day watching films for me. For all of us."

DON'T HURT DANNY KU had finished in a tie for second in the Big Eight with an 11-3 record and advanced to meet Oklahoma in the semifinals of the Big Eight tourney.

The Sooners led by four at halftime, but their troubles began when Danny Manning got hit under the right eye, a cut that required two Band-Aids to close.

Danny Manning played 4,961 minutes at KU, the most in school history by nearly 1,000 minutes.

KU QUIZ

42. Name the two football players on KU's 1988 championship basketball team.

Manning scored 27 points, and Cedric Hunter, scoreless the night before, added 18. The last time Manning had worn a Band-Aid, for a cut on the chin, he had scored a career-high 40 points against Notre Dame on Feb. 8, 1987.

"Danny plays great with Band-Aids," Brown said.

BATTLE OF THE BAND-AIDS But Band-Aids were the speciality of Missouri's Derrick Chievous. The Jayhawks met Chievous and the Tigers in the Big Eight Tournament championship. Chievous had worn a Band-Aid as a good-luck charm ever since high school.

In the championship game, Manning was wearing a big red Band-Aid on the cut under his eye, and Kevin Pritchard and MU's Lynn Hardy also sported Band-Aids for cuts on their faces.

But it was Lee Coward, who wasn't wearing a Band-Aid anywhere, who hit a 14-foot jumper in the lane with four seconds left to beat KU 67-65. Coward had also hit a 3-pointer with three seconds left on Feb. 11 to beat KU 63-60 in Columbia.

Manning scored 31 points, 21 in the second half, including 15 of KU's last 18 points. He was named the tourney's MVP.

But Chievous, with 26 points, had won the right to claim Manning's Band-Aid. And he wore it proudly on his left cheek after the game.

AT THE OMNI The KU-Missouri Big Eight tourney title game actually had little to do with NCAA seedings in 1987. Both teams knew they had made the field by the time the second half started.

KU was seeded fifth in the Southeast Regional and met Houston in the first round at the Omni in Atlanta. Using pressure defense to force 20 Houston turnovers and Kevin Pritchard's 17 points (15 in the first half), KU beat Houston 66-55. Pritchard had keyed a first-half 22-9 run with 11 straight points. The Jayhawks took a 34-21 halftime lead and never looked back.

PESKY BEARS Unranked and unheralded Southwest Missouri State had stunned No. 13 Clemson, the No. 4 seed in the Southeast Regional, 65-60 to advance to the second round of the NCAA Tournament. And Charlie Spoonhour's upset-minded Bears, appearing in their first NCAA Tournament after moving to Division I five years before, looked as if they might get their 16th straight win.

SMSU opened a 16-6 lead before Danny and the Jayhawks figured out the Bears' sticky defense. Manning took over, scoring a career-high 42 points. But it took two free throws from Chris Piper with 19 seconds remaining to seal the 67-63 win. Reserves Jeff Gueldner, Milt Newton and Scooter Barry also played key roles as KU used a smaller, quicker offense to spread out and get Manning open in the middle.

HOYAS HALT THE HAWKS The semifinal game of the NCAA Southeast Regional unfortunately went as much of KU's season had: lots of Manning and not enough anyone else.

Manning had 23 points, 19 in the first half, but no other KU player scored in double figures as Georgetown won 70-57. Cedric Hunter, with five points, was the only other Jayhawk with more than one field goal.

KU trailed by nine early in the second half, but a 10-0 run, started by a Turgeon 3-pointer, put KU ahead 41-39 with 13:26 to play. Georgetown answered with its own 13-2 run and put the game out of reach.

Hoya All-American Reggie Williams had 34 points in the only meeting ever between KU and Georgetown, and the Jayhawks were outrebounded 40-26.

Brown said after the game that he had relied on his young players to do too much. But Turgeon, whose KU playing career was over, didn't go so easy on them:

"They've got to grow up," Turgeon said of KU's youngsters. "They have a chance to win it all with Danny Manning."

1987-88: CHAMPS

There was speculation at the end of the 1986-87 season that Manning would not return for his senior year. He did, but the Jayhawks got off to a mediocre 12-8 mark that failed to inspire any thoughts of a championship or even of qualifying for the NCAA Tournament. Then KU won 15 of its final 18 games when Manning put the Jayhawks on his back and carried them all the way to a national championship with a win over Oklahoma in the title game.

Kansas became the first team with more than 10 losses to win the NCAA Tournament.

The Jayhawks had returned 10 lettermen for the 1987-88 season, including Chris Piper, Kevin Pritchard, Milt Newton, Jeff Gueldner and Archie Marshall, who had sat out a year as a medical redshirt. But they quickly faced adversity when Marshall was lost, again, in late December and starting center Marvin Branch was declared academically ineligible in mid-Janaury.

Hard to believe the season would end with rallies, a parade and a trip to the White House.

MORE TO COME KU beat Pomona-Pitzer 94-38 on Dec. 1, 1987 for its 49th straight win in Allen Fieldhouse, breaking the Big Eight record for home winning streaks. But the streak did not end there.

STARTING TO STUMBLE KU traveled to Notre Dame on Jan. 23, where David Rivers hit 29 points, including four free throws in the last 12 seconds, to beat the Jayhawks 80-76.

The road didn't get much easier as KU traveled to Lincoln three days later to face Nebraska. With the score tied at 68, Manning dribbled the ball off his leg while the Jayhawks were working for the last shot. Nebraska's Beau Reid then hit a last-second shot to beat KU 70-68.

The losses were the first back-to-back ones for the Jayhawks since their early trip to Hawaii.

THE STREAK FALLS The Jayhawks had proven unbeatable at home for 55 games, a stretch dating to Feb. 22, 1984, against Oklahoma. But on Jan. 30, 1988, Kansas State's Mitch Richmond scored 35 points and the Wildcats ended the streak. K-State pulled away late to win 72-61.

Seniors Danny Manning and Chris Piper had hoped to end their KU careers undefeated at home. And if the streak did fall, everyone assumed it would be to Oklahoma, KU's next home opponent. OU did win, 73-65, handing KU its fourth-straight loss.

"I was hoping we would get the chance to break the streak since they broke ours," OU guard Ricky Grace told the Kansan. "We just added salt to the wound. Maybe now they can start a 58-game losing streak at home."

The Jayhawks suffered one other home loss that season, against then-No. 6 Duke. The Blue Devils came back from six down in overtime to win 74-70 on Feb. 20.

ONE LAST SHOT For all practical purposes, Archie Marshall's career at KU had ended when he seriously injured his left knee on Dec. 30, 1987, against St. John's in a game that KU lost 70-56. He had already sat out a year after injuring his right knee against Duke in the NCAA semifinal game in 1986, and when Marshall got hurt against St. John's, Brown broke down on the bench. Marshall then missed the rest of the 1987-88 season. But when Oklahoma State came to Lawrence on March 5,

1988, the seniors' final home game, Brown put Marshall in the game with 1:33 remaining.

He took a 3-point shot that sailed wide of the basket.

Danny Manning drives against OU's Harvey Grant during the NCAA championship game in 1988.

K-WHO? Despite being unranked and losing to K-State in the semifinal of the Big Eight Tournament, KU was a No. 6 seed in the Midwest Regional in Lincoln, Neb. But not much was expected from the Jayhawks. KU quietly won its first-round game against No. 17 Xavier 85-72. The Jayhawks never trailed and used tough defense and 24 points from Danny Manning and 21 from Milt Newton.

In a tight second-round game against Murray State, which had upset No. 3 seed North Carolina State, Manning hit a hook shot with 37 seconds left to give KU a 59-58 lead. After the Racers tried for a final shot, Manning rebounded and added two free throws to give KU a 61-58 victory, moving the Jayhawks to the regional semifinals in Pontiac, Mich.

Ex-KU Athletic Director Monte Johnson served as the NCAA official host to Oklahoma during the 1988 Final Four.

GOIN' TO KANSAS CITY Vanderbilt had upset No. 2-seeded Pittsburgh to advance to the regional semifinals against KU. But Manning again was superb, scoring 38 points to lead the Jayhawks to a 77-64 win and a date with Kansas State in the regional final. The Wildcats had upset No. 1 seed Purdue to meet KU.

It was the fourth meeting of the year for the teams from Kansas, with K-State leading the series 2-1. But this game belonged to the Jayhawks. KU cruised to a 71-58 victory and earned a spot in the 50th Final Four, in Kansas City, Mo.

Kansas trailed early in the second half against K-State but surged behind the play of Manning, who scored 20, and Newton, who scored 18. The surprise of the game was guard Scooter Barry, who sparked the Jayhawks with a career-high 15 points.

"So many unlikely kids, who I wasn't smart enough to play earlier, stepped forward," Brown said. "They were supposed to beat us. Our kids wanted to redeem themselves."

Manning was named MVP of the Midwest Regional.

ERASING A NIGHTMARE Danny Manning had played one of his worst games against Duke during the 1986 Final Four in Dallas. The opportunity to meet the Blue Devils in the 1988 Final Four gave the All-American a chance to ease that pain.

The Jayhawks started off on a tear, running to a 14-0 lead, keyed by two 3-pointers from Milt Newton. They still led 24-6 midway through the first half, but Duke wasn't done.

The Blue Devils chipped away at the KU lead and drew within 55-52 with 4:14 remaining. The lead was still at three points when KU went on an 11-4 run to take a 10-point lead with 10 seconds to play. The Jayhawks hit 7 of 9 free throws down the stretch to clinch the 66-59 win.

Newton, continuing his tournament emergence, had contributed 20 points, and Manning had 25.

"It feels nice, but no matter what happens in this tournament, I'll always remember the '86 tournament," Manning said. "But hopefully, this dream will last a little longer."

THE FINAL REVENGE The Oklahoma Sooners had rolled through the NCAA Tournament with their run-and-gun style and arrived at the title game on April 4 as cocky as ever.

OU had won both regular-season matchups with the Jayhawks, 73-65 in Lawrence and 95-87 in Norman. And the Sooners were heavy favorites to win again after beating Arizona 86-78 in the semifinal.

Senior forward Harvey Grant made no apologies for his team's attitude.

"If the shoe was on the other foot, they'd try to beat us or embarrass us," he told the Kansan. "If we can beat

them by 100, we will. The type of team that we have, everybody wants to get their name in the book."

Conventional wisdom said KU could not play OU's style of ball and hope to win. But the Jayhawks came out running, and the teams raced to a 50-50 halftime tie, a title-game record for total points in a half.

Dave Sieger led the Sooners in the first half with six 3-pointers, and the Jayhawks shot 71 percent from the field.

In the second half, the teams played KU basketball.

The Jayhawks slowed the tempo, and Manning took over, scoring 13 points in the final 11 minutes of the game, including the four free throws in the final minute that gave KU the 83-79 win.

"This wasn't a gift," Manning said. "A lot of people said that we were lucky, but what's luck? Luck is when preparation meets opportunity."

WELCOME HOME The rally to welcome the team, originally scheduled for Allen Fieldhouse, was switched to Memorial Stadium to accomodate more people. Good move. About 30,000 were on hand to cheer the victors.

"I always wondered what this would be like," Larry Brown said to the crowd.

"It was unbelievable. You get a sense of pride when

The celebration of KU's national title was only beginning when the team gathered on the court after the game.

Danny Manning was the 1988 NCAA Tournament MVP, and Milt Newton joined him on the Final Four All-Tournament team.

Danny Manning and the Jayhawks were surprised by the size of the crowd that greeted them at Memorial Stadium the day after the title game.

you coach at Kansas because of what Phog (Allen) did and what all the other players and coaches have done, and when you are recognized like that, it's going to take a while for it to sink in."

THE CABBAGE PATCH DANCE Oklahoma's trademark in the NCAA Tournament had been its celebration dance: The Cabbage Patch.

They had danced on the bench, they had danced on the floor. They had even danced on the rims after gaining a berth into the Final Four.

But it was Kansas dancing in the end, as the team did the OU jig in front of their fans at the rally in Memorial Stadium.

"I was worried about OU dancing," Brown said. "That's what kept me awake at night. I didn't want to see those suckers dance. I wanted to see us dance."

RYAN'S LUCK Ryan Gray was the team's lucky charm in 1988. Ryan, who had an inoperable brain tumor that affected his speech and coordination, had become friends with Brown and was involved in many team activities. Unable to stand, he watched the national championship game from the stands in Kemper Arena by watching the electronic scoreboard, which displayed television shots. His mother, Kitty, also gave him some play-by-play of the final seconds.

Ryan's tumor had been discovered when he was 14 months old, and his parents had been told not to expect

him to reach the first grade. Kitty Gray said that Ryan's association with the team had helped immeasurably.

"You couldn't buy this kind of medicine for Ryan. They are absolutely the best thing that ever happened to him."

Ryan died Sept. 6, 1990, at the age of 17.

Ryan Gray was the Jayhawks' biggest fan and good-luck charm in 1988.

VERY SUPERSTITIOUS "Jimmy the bus driver" had driven the KU team around Pontiac, Mich., at the regional finals. Jimmy Dunlap, the Greyhound employee from Detroit, was flown into Kansas City during the Final Four at Brown's request.

MANNING-LESS The excitement of the national championship overshadowed the harsh reality of graduation. Danny Manning, KU's Mr. Everything, would no longer be there for the Jayhawks.

Manning went on to play for the 1988 Olympic team and was the first player chosen in the 1988 NBA draft, going to the Los Angeles Clippers.

LARRY PULLS A FAST ONE On the morning of April 8, 1988, CBS' Jim Lampley reported that Larry Brown had accepted the UCLA head coaching job.

Almost 300 fans, students, faculty members and players attended a 3 p.m. news conference that afternoon in Allen Fieldhouse, fully expecting to hear that Brown was gone. Brown looked a little stunned at the reception and said, in a somber tone: "Although I went to UCLA

The NCAA champion Jayhawks were welcomed to the White House on April 11, 1988. They presented President Reagan and first lady Nancy Reagan with NCAA championship letter jackets.

last night … I came back. And after thinking about it, I've decided to stay at the University of Kansas."

The crowd went nuts, and somewhere in Los Angeles, UCLA Athletic Director Peter Dalis went into shock. He had already scheduled a news conference for the following day to introduce Brown as his new head coach.

"When Coach Brown left Los Angeles yesterday morning, we had every reason to believe he had accepted UCLA's offer," Dalis said.

Heck, even KU Athletic Director Bob Frederick had assumed Brown was gone, learning only 30 minutes before the news conference of Brown's decision to stay.

After Brown had quieted the crowd in Allen Fieldhouse, he added only one more thought before leaving without answering questions: "I'm committed to the kids here. Like Dorothy said, there's no place like home."

VITALE SAYS ESPN analyst Dick Vitale was positive that Larry Brown would not be around for the 1988-89 season at KU. In fact, he was so sure, he staked his pride. He told a national television audience that he was so certain of Brown's departure that he would scrub the floor of Allen Fieldhouse at the first midnight scrimmage of that season if Brown were still around.

Even after Brown rejected the UCLA job, Vitale stuck by his prediction.

"To me, it's like a soap opera with Larry Brown," he said in May 1988. "You don't know what's going to happen from day to day, he's so emotional."

I'M OUTTA HERE But it wasn't emotions that finally tore Brown from KU. It was the promise of a fat paycheck back in the NBA.

On June, 13, he announced that he had accepted a $3.5 million, five-year deal, plus $1 million in bonuses, to coach the San Antonio Spurs.

This time there would be no wavering. Brown was gone, and he didn't even attend the news conference announcing his departure. He ended his career with a 135-44 record, two Final Fours and a national championship.

His five years at KU were more than he had spent at any other stop during his coaching career.

"After I made the decision not to go to UCLA and stay at Kansas," Brown said, "I had no intention to consider any other jobs.

"But the San Antonio situation presented itself, and I didn't think it would be fair to my family not to consider it. I love this place, the people and everything they did for me. It will always be special to me. I can't believe that any college coach in the country has a better situation than I did at KU."

Larry Brown waves to the fans at the parade in Lawrence to honor the Jayhawks. Two months later, he was waving good-bye, headed for San Antonio.

The real Cinderella came all the way from Disneyland to ride in a Lawrence parade honoring the national champs.

Roy Williams

Years Coached at KU: 1988-?
KU Record, through 1992: 132-37, .781 winning percentage

In just five seasons, Roy Williams has taken the Kansas program from the dark days of NCAA probation, which stemmed from recruiting violations under his predecessor, to a consistent level of excellence.

But his climb to the top level of college basketball coaching wasn't easy. Williams, a native of North Carolina, accepted a position under Coach Dean Smith at North Carolina as a part-time assistant in 1978. The job only paid only $2,700 a year, but the gamble paid off.

The job included a lot of travel across the state. He delivered footage of the North Carolina coaches' show to TV stations during football and basketball seasons, making the 504-mile round trip each Sunday.

In the summer, Williams hit the road again to sell ads to small businesses for a Tar Heel basketball calendar.

Athletic Director Bob Frederick introduced an unknown assistant coach named Roy Williams as KU's new head coach on July 8, 1988.

But Williams, who played freshman basketball at North Carolina, wasn't just logging road mileage. He was watching Smith and learning the Carolina system.

He later became a full-time assistant for Smith and eventually got his shot at being a head coach.

At the age of 37, Williams came to Kansas to replace Larry Brown, who had just guided the Jayhawks to a national title. But NCAA probation made it tough going for the new coach.

"It didn't bother me that I had to replace Larry Brown," Williams said, "but more that I had to play without Danny Manning. I knew about the investigation. They showed me the paperwork. They felt the penalties would be minor, and I agreed. It was a bad calculation."

KU QUIZ

43. Who was Roy Williams' first recruit to attend KU?

Williams' teams have won three Big Eight Conference championships and have been to two Final Fours. Only Everette Case of N.C. State won more games during his first four seasons as a head coach on the Division I level.

Williams was the Associated Press national Coach of the Year in 1992 and Big Eight Coach of the Year in 1990 and 1992.

THINKING BIG The athletic department tried to entice some established coaches to replace Brown: Mike Kryzyzewski of Duke, Gary Williams of Ohio State, Charlie Spoonhour of Southwest Missouri State, John Chaney of Temple, Bobby Cremins of Georgia Tech and Pete Gillen of Xavier.

TAKING CARE OF THE ALMA MATER Dean Smith played a large part in influencing KU officials to take a shot on Williams, a virtual unknown. Five years earlier, Smith also had helped in the hiring of Larry Brown.

"I called Dean Smith and offered him the job," said Bob Frederick, KU's athletic director, in April 1992. "I knew he'd turn it down. He said it would be hard for him to leave North Carolina after they named the arena for him."

Dean Smith didn't return to coach at his alma mater, but he's sent two of his assistants there.

ROY WHO? Many alumni were hoping for a big-name coach to step into the vacancy left by Brown. Instead, they got Williams. But Williams had picked up a few pointers from Smith.

"There's no way I can be as good as Dean Smith at anything," Williams said after getting the KU job in July 1988. "But I've been exposed to the best, and, hopefully, I'm not dumb enough not to pick up a couple of things."

Williams actually could have ended up at KU earlier than 1988. Larry Brown had asked him to be one of his assistants back in 1983, shortly after Brown arrived at KU.

"A couple of weeks later he hired Ed Manning," Williams said of Danny Manning's father. "Talk about a good choice. That's the best choice he's ever made."

ON PROBATION If Brown's exit hadn't already ended the celebration of KU's national championship, the party was

Scooter Barry, Roy Williams and Milt Newton discuss the probation at a news conference on Nov. 1, 1988.

Violations surrounding the recruitment of Vincent Askew made KU the only NCAA basketball champion that has been barred from defending its title.

officially over Nov. 1, 1988.

KU was slapped with a three-year probation stemming from 12 rules violations the NCAA uncovered during an investigation of the basketball program. The school in effect lost three scholarships for the next year, couldn't bring in recruits on paid visits for a year and, most importantly, could not defend its national title because the Jayhawks were banned from one year of postseason play.

The infractions centered on the recruitment of a transfer player, Vincent Askew of Memphis State, in June 1986. The NCAA reported that KU gave $1,244 worth of illegal inducements to Askew – including $366 that Brown gave Askew for a round-trip airline ticket to Memphis, allowing him to visit his sick grandmother.

"The kid's grandmother who raised him passed away a short time later," Brown said at the time, referring to the $366. "I'd give it to anybody if they told me his grandmother was passing away."

Because the KU football team had been placed on probation in the 1980s, KU could have been hit with the NCAA death penalty, temporarily shutting down the basketball program.

The sanctions were a difficult blow for Williams, who said in the 1989-90 KU media guide:

"When I gathered the team on Halloween the night before the announcement, to tell them of the penalties, it was probably the most difficult thing I had ever done in my life. They were the innocent ones, and they had to suffer. I know it wasn't the treat I was expecting on Halloween."

HARD FEELINGS Larry Brown took offense at being accused of running a "dirty" program, the Kansan reported on Nov. 2:

> "The thing that bothers me is that ever since I left KU, the new coach and the athletic director have been taking shots at us right from the start, and that has really troubled me because I know I left the program in pretty darn good shape."

1988-89: A ROUGH START

Williams' first team went 19-12 overall and 6-8 in the Big Eight for a sixth-place finish, KU's lowest since 1982-83. Led by senior forward Milt Newton, junior guard Kevin Pritchard and sophomore forwards Mark Randall and Mike Maddox, KU ended its season by losing to Kansas State in the first round of the Big Eight Tournament. The Jayhawks were ineligible for any further postseason play.

A TOUGH SELL Williams said in October 1988 that KU's rich basketball tradition meant little when it came to recruiting in the 1980s – a frequent complaint of former

44. Roy Williams has lost two non-conference games in Allen Fieldhouse heading into the 1993-94 season. Who were they against?

Milt Newton was the KU MVP in 1989.

Kevin Pritchard finished his KU career third on the Jayhawks' all-time assists and steals lists.

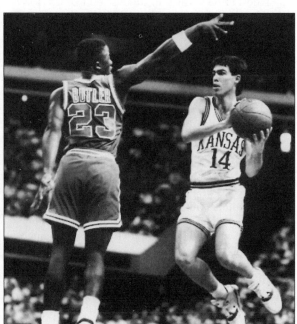

*KU lost to Missouri
91-66 on Feb. 1,
1989, the Jayhawks'
worst defeat in Allen
Fieldhouse.*

coach Larry Brown.

"If you talk to kids nowadays," Williams said, "they
think Julius Erving invented the game. They have no
idea who James Naismith is."

POURING IT ON Not a lot had been expected from the
Jayhawks, and they surprised most people by jumping to
a 13-1 record. KU broke the 100-point barrier six times
during those first 14 games. And in Williams' first Big
Eight game, the Jayhawks set a new school record for
points scored by beating Iowa State 127-82 on Jan. 7.
The previous mark of 121 points had been set against
Central Missouri State in 1977. Nine Jayhawks finished
the Iowa State game in double figures, another school
record.

HITTING THE SKIDS KU climbed as high as No. 16 in the
Associated Press poll, but after a 16-3 start, the Jayhawks
slumped. They lost eight straight as injuries and the
tough part of their schedule kicked in.

Not in 41 years, since the 1947-48 season, had a KU
team lost so many games in a row. The slump included
four straight losses in Allen Fieldhouse, the longest
home losing streak since 1962-63.

*45. How many 3-
pointers did Mark
Randall make during
his career at
Kansas?*

1,400 WINS When KU finally did win again, beating
Colorado 111-83 at Allen Fieldhouse on Feb. 25, 1989,
the Jayhawks did more than put an end to the losing
streak. It was the 1,400th win for Kansas, making it only
the third school to hit that milestone. The others were
Kentucky and North Carolina.

BOOS FOR LARRY Danny Manning and Larry Brown
dropped by Allen Fieldhouse to watch KU's final home
game against Nebraska on March 1, 1989. KU won the
game 80-71 despite sloppy play.

The appearance of Manning and Brown brought out a
lot of emotions – some of them negative.

"A scattering of boos greeted Brown, the former
Jayhawk coach who left KU with an NCAA probation as
well as a national title, when he took his seat in the
stands," the Wichita Eagle reported.

"Brown, who had the night off from his slumping San
Antonio Spurs, drew a few more boos when (he) was
introduced during a time-out early in the first half.

"The P.A. announcer, however, quickly followed by
introducing Manning, silencing the boos as the crowd
cheered the former KU All-American."

1989-90: RISING TO THE TOP

Williams and the Jayhawks rebounded for the 1989-90 season, finishing 30-5 overall and 11-3 in the Big Eight, tied for second. The team returned Pritchard, Randall, Maddox, Freeman West and Jeff Gueldner. But several first-year players made an impact as well: Terry Brown, Adonis Jordan, Alonzo Jamison, Pekka Markkanen and Rick Calloway. The Jayhawks' season ended with a second-round NCAA Tournament loss to UCLA.

Kevin Pritchard was an All-Big Eight selection in 1990.

FAST START IN NIT The 1989-90 Jayhawks were picked to finish anywhere from fourth to eighth in the Big Eight. Kevin Pritchard didn't buy it.

"We won't come in eighth," he said. "I'll put my basketball up if we come in eighth."

After dismantling Alabama-Birmingham at home in the opening round of the Dodge NIT preseason tournament, KU upset No. 2 LSU 89-83 in Baton Rouge La., to advance to the semifinals in New York City's Madison Square Garden. KU used its unselfish passing game to overcome the size of LSU, which had 7-footers Shaquille O'Neal and Stanley Roberts.

The Jayhawks, led by tourney MVP Mark Randall, defeated No. 1 and eventual national champion UNLV

Roy Williams was named the national Coach of the Year in 1990 by the United States Basketball Writers' Association.

"Downtown" Terry Brown ranks No. 1 on KU's all-time 3-point list, having made 200 in his career.

Mark Randall, who played in 1987 and from 1989 to 1991, finished his career at No. 6 on the school's all-time scoring and rebounding lists.

91-77 in the semifinals and St. Johns 66-57 in the tournament final. The previously unranked Jayhawks shot up to No. 4 in the nation.

BREAKFAST AT ROY'S The most difficult NCAA penalty, Williams said in a Wichita Eagle story in November, 1989, was the one preventing any paid campus visits for recruits until Dec. 31, 1989:

> "'I can think of five players we really wanted who decided not to consider us because we couldn't pay for their visits.'
>
> "Williams can't even buy a recruit a Coke at McDonald's.
>
> "Just last weekend, Williams served breakfast at his home to two recruits, then had to charge the prospects $3 each for the meals. He turned the six bucks over to the athletic department.

KENTUCKY KO'D KU routed Kentucky 150-95 on Dec. 9 in Lawrence. Led by "Downtown" Terry Brown's 7-for-10 shooting beyond the 3-point stripe and 31 points, the Jayhawks broke school records for most points in a game (150), most points in one half (80), and most assists (36).

BEACH BALL Before their game in Miami on Jan. 10, 1990, which KU won 100-73, the Jayhawks mixed business with pleasure, practicing for the Hurricanes on a South Florida beach. Williams had the team managers draw a "court" in the sand, and KU then walked through its drills to prepare for Miami's offense.

"They would have probably liked it more if we had practiced in the middle of the day," Williams said. "There may have been more pretty girls out there."

MORE OF LARRY'S BAGGAGE KU had some stinkers on its schedule during Williams' first few seasons. He inherited five Division II games from Brown. The scheduling mismatches included Elizabeth City State, an NCAA Division II school in North Carolina.

According to the Wichita Eagle, "Part of the baggage of bringing Ed (Manning) included paying back Ed's old friends, one of whom is C.J. Mackey," who coached Elizabeth City State.

KU tried to back out of the scheduled game in 1990, but Elizabeth City was to receive $14,000 for the game — a huge chunk of the school's basketball budget.

TRIBUTE Midway through the season, the Jayhawks began wearing No. 22 marked on their shoes as a tribute to KU recruit Chris Lindley. That was Lindley's jersey number at Raytown South High in Kansas City, Mo. Lindley, who had signed a letter of intent to play at KU, had lost his right foot in an accident. He later attended KU on an institutional scholarship.

WHO'S NO. 1? KU took a 19-0 record and a No. 1 ranking to Columbia on Jan. 20 to face No. 4 Missouri. But four Tigers scored at least 20 points, led by Anthony Peeler's 24, as Missouri beat KU 95-87 to end the Jayhawks' streak and take over the No. 1 ranking.

The Jayhawks then won five straight Big Eight games before meeting Mizzou again, this time on Feb. 13 in Allen Fieldhouse. KU had climbed back over the Tigers to the No. 1 spot in the nation after MU lost to Kansas State. Kansas fans were hoping for revenge in the

In 1989-90, four players had more than 100 assists, and Kansas finished the season with the highest field-goal percentage in the nation.

The hype surrounding the nationally televised KU-Missouri rematch on Feb. 13, 1990, was intense. Students started camping out for seats on the Wednesday before the Monday game.

The Jayhawks weren't in the Final Four in 1990, but KU guards Jeff Gueldner and Kevin Pritchard went to Denver, the site of the Final Four, anyway. Pritchard competed in the All-Star Game, and Gueldner won the 3-point shooting contest.

The Jayhawks watch their Big Eight Tournament semifinal game against Oklahoma slip away on March 10, 1990. From left to right: Pekka Markanen, Mike Maddox, Mark Randall and Kevin Pritchard.

Missouri-Kansas rematch, but the Tigers won 77-71 and again regained the No. 1 spot.

Missouri then fell to Oklahoma 107-90 in Norman, and KU was back at No. 1. But the Jayhawks' trip to Oklahoma didn't go much better as KU suffered its worst loss of the season, 100-78. Oklahoma then moved into the No. 1 spot, the third Big Eight team to hold the top ranking that season.

BREAKING THE JINX The Jayhawks headed for Iowa State and the dreaded Hilton Coliseum in Ames on Feb. 10, 1990. They hadn't won there since 1983, a six-game losing streak that had claimed some of KU's most dominant teams. But the Hilton Magic was all used up, and the Jayhawks won 88-83 behind Kevin Pritchard's 18 points and seven assists. "I was reading the paper the other day, and it said that Larry Brown never won here," Pritchard said. "Well, Larry didn't, but this team did."

CRASH LANDING IN NCAAs A season that started with no expectations had quickly fostered high hopes. But it ended in disappointment. KU was the second seed in the East Regional in Atlanta and won its first-round game against Robert Morris 79-71. That set up a second-round match with UCLA. Three of the Bruins' previous wins over KU had come in NCAA play.

So did the fourth.

Two free throws by UCLA's Tracy Murray put UCLA

up 71-70, but KU had one last shot. Rick Calloway's 15-footer bounced off the rim, and Jeff Gueldner's follow-up was swatted by the Bruins' Don MacLean.

The Jayhawks finished at 30-5, the second-most wins in KU history. But Williams did not take the loss well, choking back tears as he said, "These guys played so well for so long that, at times, they made me feel inadequate as a coach."

KU QUIZ

46. Which Jayhawk holds the record for most steals in a game?

TOO MUCH PRESSURE Reflecting on the loss to UCLA, Williams said that the pressure had gotten to the team:

> "Last year's team felt so much pressure. They didn't enjoy Atlanta one bit.
>
> "They accomplished so much during the season, and so much was expected. They were so conscientious. They worried about what Mom and Dad thought, what their girlfriends thought, what the janitor thought."

HOME TO FINLAND On April 9, 1990, KU center Pekka Markkanen announced he would not return for his senior season. Markkanen said he had decided to return to his hometown of Jyvaskyla, Finland.

1990-91: AN IMPROBABLE RUN

Roy Williams never saw Pekka Markkanen play before he arrived at KU.

KU's 1990-91 team finished 27-8 overall and 10-4 in the Big Eight for a share of the league title, but it was the Jayhawks' magical NCAA Tournament stretch that highlighted the season. After winning its first two regional games, KU rolled past No. 3 Indiana, No. 2 Arkansas and No. 4 North Carolina before meeting Duke in the title game. Seniors Mark Randall, Terry Brown, Mike Maddox and Kirk Wagner provided experience for a team that also included junior Alonzo Jamison, sophomore Adonis Jordan and freshmen Richard Scott and Steve Woodberry.

MIRACLE RECOVERY Mark Randall had surgery in late November for a muscle injury in his lower right calf. He was expected to miss anywhere from 10 days to four weeks. But only four days after surgery, Randall returned to action, coming off the bench to help KU win its home opener against Marquette, 108-71.

Starter Mike Maddox played with intense back pain for much of the 1990-91 season.

GET A WATCH Early in the 1990-91 season, starting guard Adonis Jordan seemed to have a penchant for missing various forms of transportation ... and making Williams mad. First, Jordan was benched for the first half of the Maryland-Baltimore County game for missing the team flight from Norman, Okla. He hadn't learned his lesson, though, and didn't play in the game at Oklahoma State after he missed the team bus.

Jordan's absence at the OSU game was key. KU lost in overtime after Sean Tunstall missed two free throws with the score tied and two seconds left in regulation. The Jayhawks were 0-2 to start Big Eight play.

Alonzo Jamison was known as the defensive specialist for the Jayhawks and would usually pick up the toughest defensive assignment for Roy Williams. Jamison holds the KU record for steals in a game (8), setting the mark against Marquette on Dec. 1, 1990, in Lawrence. He also had eight Jan. 2, 1992, against Pepperdine.

KU QUIZ

47. What do Rex Walters and Wilt Chamberlain have in common?

TROUBLE WITH THE HUSKERS On March 3, 1991, KU went to Lincoln needing to beat Nebraska to claim the Big Eight title outright. But the Jayhawks committed 20 turnovers in the first half and trailed by 13 points at the intermission. They never recovered, losing 85-75 to settle for a co-championship with Oklahoma State. Ranked No. 12 heading into the Big Eight Tournament, KU dispensed of Colorado in the first round, 82-76, as Mark Randall led four Jayhawks in double figures.

But the semifinals brought a rematch with Nebraska, and the Cornhuskers won a foul-filled game 87-83. Williams was openly bitter after the game:

"I felt totally helpless," Williams told the Kansan. "I don't want to take anything away from Nebraska or the great feelings they are enjoying right now to comment on three incompetent men who felt they had to be dictators out on the court."

FRESH START KU was named the No. 3 seed in the Southeast Regional and defeated New Orleans 54-49 in a defensive battle, then dropped Pittsburgh 77-66 to advance to the Sweet 16.

CANCEL THE RESERVATIONS Indiana was seeded second in the Southeast Regional, ranked third in the country and was fully expected to battle for the national title at home in Indianapolis, the site of the Final Four. KU met the Hoosiers on March 21 in the regional semifinal game in Charlotte, N.C.

Kansas streaked to a 26-6 lead, sparked by Terry Brown's 3-point shooting. The Jayhawks slowed the tempo and never let Indiana make a run in the second half. KU won 83-65 to advance to the regional final.

"The referee came over about five minutes into the game and said there was a screw loose in the floor," Hoosier coach Bob Knight said at the news conference after the game. "I said to him, 'Then why don't we start this again tomorrow?' I think that was the best suggestion I had in the entire first half."

ON TO INDY Nolan Richardson's physical Arkansas Razorbacks had used the phrase "Forty Minutes of Hell" as their rallying cry all season. And for the Jayhawks, the first 20 minutes of their meeting with Arkansas in the Southeast Regional final must have felt a lot like that. KU, stunned as Arkansas' Todd Day hit 21 points, trailed by 12 points at the half.

"All I did at halftime was ask them to do what they

48. To commemorate basketball's 100th anniversary in 1991, KU announced the retirement of eight jerseys. What are the jersey numbers and to whom do they belong?

Bob Knight is 0-3 against Roy Williams.

Adonis Jordan, shown driving down the floor during KU's upset of Arkansas in the 1991 Southeast Regional final, took the Jayhawks to two Final Fours as the team's floor leader. He is KU's No. 3 all-time assists leader with 568.

Alonzo Jamison played most of the 1990-91 season with torn cartilage in his right shoulder. Despite nagging pain, he shot 59.5 percent from the field.

were asked to do, do what they're supposed to do, and things will work out fine," Williams said after the game.

They listened. Sparked by the Southeast Regional MVP Alonzo Jamison, the Jayhawks came back. Kansas took its first lead with nine minutes to play, and the Razorbacks never led again as KU won 93-81 to advance to the Final Four.

ROWDY WELCOME When the Jayhawks returned from Charlotte near midnight on March 23, about 5,000 fans greeted them at Forbes Field in Topeka. Nice. But nothing compared with the 14,000 who had gathered at Allen Fieldhouse back in Lawrence. The raucous crowd went nuts when the team came onto the floor.

Even Williams seemed a little caught up in the moment:

"There are a lot of things we keep in the family, that we don't tell the press. But I'm going to let you in on a secret. Before the game, I told the team it wasn't going to be 40 minutes of hell – it was going to be 80, because we were going to be there, too."

ROY'S BOYS Without any star players, Williams and the "North Carolina system" got a lot of attention when KU advanced to the Final Four. But Williams was quick to pass the credit back to the players at a news conference in Lawrence before leaving for Indianapolis:

"It's not the Carolina system, it's not some Boy Wonder sitting on the bench. It's kids who have 'Kansas' on their jerseys, who have played their tails off."

RANDALL'S RING Mark Randall was given a national championship ring for KU's national title in 1988. But he vowed that he would never wear it. Instead, it was buried in his mother's safe-deposit box in Denver.

Randall was forced to watch the 1988 title game from the bench in a suit and tie, having been given a medical redshirt to correct a breathing and jaw alignment ailment.

Mark Randall has KU's highest career field-goal percentage at 62 percent.

"It was a special thing, and I'm fortunate enough to say I was along," Randall said later. "But I didn't step on the floor and have the satisfaction of playing. Even if it was just a pass or a screen, I would have felt I did something. I practiced with them and can feel I helped in that sense.

"But I'll never touch the ring. It'll be out, and people can look at it. But it won't be on my hand."

STUDENT VS. TEACHER On March 30, after days of hype surrounding the matchup between Williams and his mentor, KU and UNC met in the Hoosier Dome in

It was high fives all around as the Jayhawks celebrated their victory against Arkansas, which secured a spot in the 1991 Final Four.

Roy Williams and North Carolina coach Dean Smith visit before their national semifinal game at the 1991 Final Four.

Indianapolis.

Both teams went through spurts in the first half, with KU taking a 43-34 lead into the locker room. North Carolina had cut the lead to 58-57, but a 9-0 KU streak, sparked by a 3-pointer from Sean Tunstall and layups from Jordan and Richard Scott, put KU in control at 65-57 with 5:31 in the game.

But the most vivid memory of the game came when Dean Smith was ejected with 35 seconds remaining after collecting his second technical foul. As Smith left the floor, he congratulated the KU players, who won 79-73.

OUT-DUKED While KU was on its own unbelievable run, Duke had pulled off what many thought was simply impossible when the Blue Devils upset No. 1 and previously unbeaten UNLV 79-77 to advance to the title game.

Duke was in its fifth Final Four in six years and had never won the title. This time the Blue Devils would not be denied. Duke jumped out early and never trailed. A late Kansas rally cut Duke's 14-point lead to five with 45 seconds left, but it was too late, and KU lost 72-65.

Duke's Christian Laettner had 18 points and 10 rebounds, Mark Randall and Billy McCaffrey scored 16 points in 26 minutes. Randall led the Jayhawks with 18 points, but Richard Scott and Alonzo Jamison were a combined 4 of 19 from the field.

"We came out flat and never seemed to get into the game," Jamison said. "How much does it hurt? I can't even answer that question."

WELCOME HOME About 12,000 fans greeted the national runners-up in Memorial Stadium the day after their loss. The rally was a celebration of a surprising season and a great tournament run. The players, according to the Wichita Eagle, "trudged off the bus at Memorial Stadium, heads and shoulders slumped. Exhausted mentally and physically."

But the rally seemed to lighten their spirits.

The biggest roar from the crowd came after Williams "took a poke at his predecessor, Larry Brown."

"The last time there was this kind of celebration here, it was after KU won the title, and two months later the coach was gone," he said. "I'd like to be here for several

Duke's Billy McCaffrey battles KU's Adonis Jordan, left, and Terry Brown for the ball during the 1991 NCAA championship game. McCaffrey's hot shooting sparked the Blue Devils and ended KU's title hopes.

KU wasn't expected to make it to the national championship game in 1991. But that didn't make the postgame news conference any easier for Roy Williams and Adonis Jordan after the Jayhawks lost.

more of these. So if you don't mind, I'd like to stay around."

REFLECTING ON THE LOSS As with any loss, Williams took the defeat to Duke pretty hard:

"I told the kids not to let that last game take away from the whole season," he said. "I'm having trouble following my own advice. It does hurt a great deal.

"That last couple of weeks, I really thought we could win the whole doggone thing. That last two weeks was an amazing ride. I'd just have liked to have made one more lap."

1991-92: BIG PLANS FALL FLAT

After the amazing run to the Final Four in 1991, expectations for the 1991-92 season were soaring at KU. Senior forward Alonzo Jamison led a tourney-savvy team that included Rex Walters, Adonis Jordan, Eric Pauley, Patrick Richey, Richard Scott and Steve Woodberry. And the Jayhawks lived up to their billing for most of the season, claiming the conference title and winning KU's first Big Eight Tournament championship since 1986.

But the bottom fell out when the Jayhawks, after trouncing Howard in the opening round, fell to UTEP in the second round of the NCAA Tournament.

Adonis Jordan was named to the All-Big Eight first team in 1992.

CARDINALS CRASH THE PARTY KU started the season winning its first 11 games. But Louisville visited Lawrence on Jan. 11, 1992, and won 85-78. The

Cardinals handed KU its first loss and ended a 24-game winning streak in Allen Fieldhouse.

BREAKING THE OU JINX KU got its first win at Oklahoma since 1986 by upending the Sooners 96-95 on Feb. 1, 1992. Rex Walters led the Jayhawks with 24 points, but Alonzo Jamison was the hero, collecting 23 points and eight assists. He also sank 3 of 4 free throws down the stretch to seal the win.

GRUDGE MATCH The battle for the conference race came down to Oklahoma State and Kansas. The teams' first meeting of the season saw the nation's No. 2 team, OSU, beat the No. 3 Jayhawks 64-56 in Stillwater on Feb. 8. Fifty-two fouls were called in an ugly, physical game, but KU hit only 30 percent from the line as Sean Sutton scored 16 points to key the Cowboys' victory.

BUZZER-BEATERS On Feb. 19, 1992, KU traveled to Lincoln to meet Nebraska. The Jayhawks trailed by as

Rex Walters transferred to KU from Northwestern in 1990 after his sophomore year. He had originally been interested in playing for the Jayhawks out of high school in San Jose, Calif. But KU coach Larry Brown wasn't interested in recruiting Walters.

Steve Woodberry led Wichita South to two state championships during his high-school career.

many as 15 points in the first half. But KU battled back to take the game to overtime, where Nebraska's sophomore point guard Jamar Johnson hit a fade-away 3-pointer from the corner as the buzzer sounded. The Huskers had beaten the No. 3 Jayhawks 81-79.

Three days later, KU was on the other end of a buzzer-beating shot as Steve Woodberry hit a running 15-footer to beat Kansas State 54-52 in Manhattan. The win moved KU to 20-3 overall and 8-2 in the Big Eight. It was the Wildcats' ninth straight loss against the Jayhawks in Manhattan.

TITLE CLINCHER On March 2, 1992, the Jayhawks' 77-64 win over Oklahoma State gave KU at least a share of the Big Eight title. The Jayhawks, in avenging one of their three losses, outrebounded Oklahoma State 41-26, including a 25-8 advantage in the first half. KU finished with a season-high 20 offensive rebounds and was led by Rex Walters' 18 points, including 10 straight during a crucial stretch.

The Jayhawks could have claimed the title outright themselves with a victory against Iowa State, but they lost 70-66 in Ames. Oklahoma helped out, however, beating Missouri 81-67, giving KU its first outright title since 1985-86.

AIR PEELER The Jayhawks used a balanced team effort to overcome a stunning performance by Anthony Peeler when Missouri came to Lawrence to wrap up the Big Eight season on March 8, 1992. Peeler made the most of his last game against the Jayhawks, scoring 19 of his career-high 43 points in the final 7 1/2 minutes. KU off-set that with six players in double figures to win 97-89 and claim the Big Eight title by three games.

In a Kansas City Star story, Roy Williams said he was impressed by Peeler: "I told Anthony I have worked with Michael Jordan and James Worthy and Sam Perkins and Brad Daugherty and 14 first-round draft choices, and I've never seen any of them put on a better exhibition than his today."

After the game, the Jayhawks celebrated their title. The senior players addressed the crowd, wearing championship hats and T-shirts. The Big Eight trophy was awarded, and the nets came down.

Roy Williams had high praise for Anthony Peeler after he scored 43 points against KU in 1992.

BIG EIGHT TOURNEY TITLE At the Big Eight Tournament, Rex Walters scored 19 points as KU beat Colorado 84-66 in the first round to give Roy Williams his 100th coaching victory. Then the bench came through in the Jayhawks' second-round 85-67 victory over Oklahoma to send KU to the final to face Oklahoma State.

Oklahoma State was ranked No. 11 heading into the final and controlled the tempo to take a 21-20 halftime lead as KU shot a dismal 32 percent from the field. But the Jayhawks got things straightened out during the intermission and went 15 of 21 from the field (71 percent) in the second half to win 66-57 and move to 26-4 on the season. The victory gave KU its first conference tourney title since 1986 and a No. 1 seed in the NCAA Midwest Regional. The Big Eight had six teams in the NCAA field: KU, Oklahoma State, Missouri, Oklahoma, Nebraska and Iowa State.

MVP SNUB Byron Houston was named the Most Valuable Player of the conference tourney after scoring 62 points and grabbing 31 rebounds. But Williams didn't exactly agree with the choice.

"I love Byron Houston to death," Williams said. "But somebody in the Kansas locker room should have been MVP."

Williams said his vote would have been for Walters, who scored 51 points and hit 22 of 23 free throws in the tourney.

RAN OFF THE ROAD The Jayhawks' path to the Final Four looked simple as the NCAA Tournament began. As the No. 1 seed at the Midwest sub-regional in Dayton, Ohio, all KU had to do was win its first two rounds to advance to the regional semifinals in Kansas City's Kemper Arena, where the Jayhawks were already 5-0 that season.

Things started just as planned, with KU beating Howard 100-67 in the first round. The game set Jayhawk NCAA Tournament records for most points (previous record 96, vs. Michigan State, 1986), and widest margin of victory (previous 25, vs. North Carolina A&T, 1986), and the 32 assists were the most ever by a team in a Midwest Regional and fourth in NCAA Tournament history. Freshman center Greg Ostertag led the Jayhawks with 16 points in 12 minutes as KU shot 61 percent from the field.

Greg Ostertag, at 7 feet 2, is the tallest player on record to ever play for Kansas. He has a reach of 9 feet 6.

But the Jayhawks should have saved some of that shooting touch for later. A second-round matchup with No. 9 seed Texas-El Paso brought a stunning 66-60 defeat, ending the KU season about two weeks earlier than anyone expected.

Don Haskins had coached UTEP back in 1966 when

Kansas has never beaten UCLA (0-8), Michigan (0-5) or Texas-El Paso (0-3).

the Miners won it all after beating Jo Jo White and KU. This time, Haskins' team used a spread offense, taking 35 to 40 seconds on most possessions in the second half and shooting 58 percent from the field. Walters had 14 points for KU and UTEP's Johnny Melvin had 18 points, including two free throws with 13 seconds remaining to clinch the win.

"I can't say how much I feel the hurt for these guys," Williams said after the game. "They accomplished so much. But the nature of the game is that people will say this season has been a disappointment because of the loss. I'm disappointed with the loss, but I'm not disappointed in our kids."

WHAT HAPPENED? At his end-of-the-season news conference, Williams blamed the loss to UTEP partially on the fact that he let the Jayhawks watch the Miners' first-round win over Evansville, breaking his own rule.

"I go out to scout the game, and some of my players come out to watch it," Williams said. "Dumb old Roy said, 'They can handle it.' If you ask our players, they looked at the game and figured they could beat those guys. They looked past UTEP in some ways, and we've never done that here."

1992-93: BAYOU-BOUND

Determined to erase the memories of the loss to UTEP, Kansas began the 1992-93 season highly touted and led by its senior backcourt tandem of Walters and Jordan. Senior Eric Pauley and juniors Steve Woodberry, Richard Scott and Darrin Hancock also were to play key roles. But the transfer of sophomore forward Ben Davis, injuries to several players and inconsistent play brought doubts as the season progressed. KU overcame all that to finish 29-7 overall and 11-3 in the Big Eight for KU's third-straight conference title. The Jayhawks advanced to their fourth Final Four in eight years, losing to North Carolina in the semifinals.

Richard Scott was named to the 1993 All-Midwest Regional team.

FINAL FOUR IN DECEMBER Kansas, ranked third in the country, traveled to Indianapolis to meet the No. 2 Indiana Hoosiers on Dec. 5, 1992, having already beaten Georgia earlier in the week. The Jayhawks hung on to beat Indiana 74-69. The nationally televised game was part of a weekend that also saw No. 1 Michigan lose to No. 4 Duke.

Adonis Jordan and Steve Woodberry shot a combined

10 for 10 from the free-throw line to keep the Jayhawks in the game despite a nine-minute field-goal drought against Indiana. Free-throw shooting proved important as KU went 15 of 20 from the line and Indiana hit only 3 of 15. Jordan and Walters had 16 points each, with Walters driving the lane for an acrobatic shot that gave KU a 72-69 lead late, and Jordan hitting the two free throws that iced the game.

KU is 6-0 in regional final games in the NCAA Tournament.

CLASSIC ENCOUNTER Kansas was 7-0 and ranked No. 2 when the Jayhawks traveled to the Islands for the Rainbow Classic in Honolulu. In the first round, KU survived Lindsey Hunter's 48 points (including 11 3-pointers) to beat Jackson State 93-85. The second round brought an easy 94-66 win over host Hawaii, setting up a meeting with No. 6 Michigan and its highly touted Fab Five (Chris Webber, Jalen Rose, Jimmy King, Ray Jackson and Juwan Howard). The Wolverines had squeaked by North Carolina on a last-second shot to advance to the final on Dec. 31. Michigan was just too

KU's dynamic back-court duo of Rex Walters and Adonis Jordan, shown after KU beat California in the NCAA Tournament, lived up to their preseason hype. They led KU to the Final Four and were considered the best guard tandem in the nation.

much for KU inside, and the Jayhawks couldn't hit from outside. The Wolverines won 86-74, handing KU its first loss of the season.

"They outscrapped us, outplayed us, outcoached us, maybe everything you can do," Williams said after the game.

O-R-U KIDDING? On Jan. 14, KU met Oral Roberts in Allen Fieldhouse and trounced the Titans 140-72, the second-biggest victory margin in school history. Seven players scored in double figures, led by Patrick Richey's career-high 23.

"I don't have any problems with the score," said ORU coach Ken Trickey. "We didn't have any business being in Lawrence, Kansas, tonight."

1,500 AND COUNTING On Jan. 16, KU met Louisville on the road, winning 98-77 to vault from No. 4 to No. 1 in the AP poll. Walters and Jordan each made 4 of 5 3-pointers, and the Jayhawks shot 65 percent from the field to claim the 1,500th victory in school history.

BEACHED AT HOME Riding a seven-game winning streak, the No. 1 Jayhawks met Long Beach State in Lawrence on Jan. 25, 1993. The 49ers were coming off a 34-point loss to Virginia Commonwealth. But led by the 24 points of Lucious Harris, Adonis Jordan's high school team-mate, Long Beach State upset the Jayhawks 64-49. KU shot only 42 percent from the field and collected only five assists on 22 field goals. The last time KU had fewer assists in a game was in Ted Owens' final season. The loss cost the Jayhawks their No. 1 ranking and frustrated Williams.

"Everything that could go wrong did go wrong," Williams told the Kansan. "I'm sorry I can't analyze it anymore, but we got our butts kicked."

BEATING THE SPREAD UTEP and Long Beach State were successful at spreading out their offenses to beat the Jayhawks, but they were not the only teams to try it. Williams, sounding downright defensive, was quick to point that out:

"To say we can't beat a spread offense is a bunch of garbage. We've only faced it about 25 times in the last two years, and we're 23-2 against it."

ROUGH TIMES Inconsistencies plagued the Jayhawks in February and early March. The team, which had played so well in early January and had been ranked No. 1, had become suspect, finishing a lackluster 9-5 heading into the NCAA Tournament. The second loss of the stretch was another squeaker in Lincoln, Neb., against the Cornhuskers on Feb. 7, 1993. KU had its chances down the stretch, but NU held on for the 68-64 victory.

KU bounced back with victories against Oklahoma State and Missouri, beating the Tigers at the Hearnes Center for the third straight year.

But then Kansas was outgunned by Oklahoma on Feb. 17, 1993, 80-77 at Allen Fieldhouse. It was KU's second loss at home and the only loss that season to a team that did not make the NCAA tourney.

KU followed the loss with another victory against K-State. But with Eric Pauley on the bench nursing a bum left knee, the Jayhawks dropped their game against Iowa State in Ames, losing 75-71.

STEALING THE SHOW On March 4, Nebraska visited Allen Fieldhouse for the final home game of the season, where the seniors are traditionally honored. But it was a junior, Steve Woodberry, who led the Jayhawks with 26 points as they clinched their third-straight Big Eight title, beating the Huskers 94-83.

During his junior season, Steve Woodberry was touted as the best sixth man in college basketball.

Kansas has met
Missouri and Kansas
State more times
than any other oppo-
nent (226 times
each, heading into
the 1993-94 season).

K-STATE BREAKS THE HEX The Jayhawks opened the Big
Eight Tournament with an 82-65 win over Colorado that
wasn't as simple as the score indicated. KU actually
trailed by 11 points with 14 minutes to play before the
Jayhawks slapped on their swarming press, keying a 20-3
run.

But the scare from the Buffs was not enough to jolt
the Jayhawks out of their stupor. The second round
brought the third meeting of the season between KU and
Kansas State.

KU had won both regular-season meetings. But this
time Kansas State rallied from a 63-56 deficit to take a
73-65 lead with 28 seconds to play. The Wildcats held
on to upset the No. 7 Jayhawks 74-67. It broke an eight-
game losing streak to the Jayhawks and was K-State
coach Dana Altman's first victory against KU.

Vince Jackson led the Wildcats with 25 points and
seven rebounds, but Anthony Beane hit a key 3-pointer
late. Adonis Jordan, hampered by a painful stress fracture
in his left leg, was unable to guard Beane closely, but the
Jayhawks weren't making excuses.

K-State's Anthony
Beane, shown dri-
ving against KU's
Calvin Rayford,
scored 19 points in
the 1993 Big Eight
Tournament semi-
final game.

"If we play Kansas State 10 times, we should be able to beat them 10 times," Rex Walters said after the game.

MEETING OF THE MINDS The day after the loss to Kansas State, the Kansas players and coaches held a team meeting to get things straightened out. No one wanted a repeat of the UTEP game in the tourney.

"Let's just say we had lost some of our focus and we needed to challenge ourselves and each other in a direct way," Jordan said. "We didn't want it to happen again. We didn't want to do what we did last year."

THE RODNEY DANGERFIELD JAYHAWKS Despite being the No. 2 seed in the Midwest Regional, Kansas wasn't getting much respect heading into the tournament and many analysts forecast an early exit for the Jayhawks.

KU faced a tough Ball State club in the first round. But the upset didn't happen, as KU dismantled the No. 15 seed in the second half. The Jayhawks outscored Ball State 34-14 in the final seven minutes on their way to a 94-72 victory at the Rosemont Horizon in Rosemont, Ill. Rex Walters led the Jayhawks with 23 points, making all six of his 3-point attempts.

KU shot 50 percent from the field for the first time in more than a month.

The Jayhawks' second-round opponent, BYU, hung tough and held on to a 68-67 lead late in the game. Then came the KU surge. Sparked by Rex Walters and his career-high 28 points, the Jayhawks went on a 19-2 run with 4 1/2 minutes left to knock out the Cougars 90-76.

KU AND THE KIDD KU was on track to face Duke in the Sweet 16 at The Arena in St. Louis, Mo. But it didn't happen.

The California Bears, led by their superstar freshman guard Jason Kidd, upset the two-time defending champs in the second round. Kidd, who opted to attend school in his home state instead of attending KU, had played brilliantly in the tourney.

But when the Jayhawks and Bears met, KU pulled away late for a 93-76 victory after being down early in the second half and earned a spot in the regional final against Indiana.

Walters and Jordan combined for 39 points on 13-of-18 shooting (including 7 of 9 from outside the 3-point arc).

KU iced the victory by hitting 17 of its last 19 free throws.

KU QUIZ

49. Name the five KU players who have ended their careers with more than 1,300 points and 600 rebounds.

INDIANA REMATCH A trip to the Final Four came down to a rematch of teams that had met in December: KU and Indiana.

The Jayhawks faced the task of beating Bob Knight's Hoosiers again. No coach outside the Big Ten had ever beaten a Knight-coached team twice in the same season.

Until Roy Williams came along.

Kansas came out shooting well and playing tough defense and led at halftime 38-34.

Indiana, which was playing without forward Alan Henderson, who injured his knee late in the season, regained the lead 50-48 with 12:52 left to play. But KU answered with a 10-0 run.

Late in the game, Indiana rallied to cut the KU lead to 76-73. The momentum appeared to be shifting in Indiana's favor. But Walters quickly took the inbound pass down the sideline and completed a tricky cross-court bounce pass to a streaking Adonis Jordan. Jordan's layup pushed the KU lead back to five. Free throws and tough defense capped off the upset as KU won 83-77, sending Williams to his second Final Four.

All five KU starters scored in double figures, led by forward Richard Scott's 16 points.

KU celebrates after beating Indiana to win the Midwest Regional and earn a berth in its second Final Four under Roy Williams.

Senior Adonis Jordan claimed a piece of the net in St. Louis after KU won the Midwest Regional final.

Indiana's All-American Calbert Cheaney, playing in his final collegiate game, scored 22 points and was named the regional's MVP. But KU's swarming defense got to him.

"They kept running in three or four guys every five or six minutes," Cheaney said after the game. "Every time I came off a screen, they had somebody waiting for me."

JAY-HAWKERS Was it their swarming defense and hot shooting that got the Jayhawks back to the Final Four, or was it spit? Superstitious Roy Williams started the ritual of having the team spit in the Mississippi River for good luck before games in St. Louis. He said it was something he did as a part-time assistant at North Carolina in 1982 when the Tar Heels won the national championship in New Orleans. Kansans were whipped into a spitting frenzy, doing their part to give the Hawks a little more luck.

But that wasn't the only superstition used by the coach. Another Williams' good luck tactic: to visit the grave sites of James Naismith and Phog Allen in Lawrence, Kan., and pat their tombstones.

HEELS AND HAWKS The Jayhawks had advanced to New Orleans and another Final Four matchup with North Carolina, again pitting Roy Williams against his mentor, Dean Smith. This time, Smith came out on top as 7-footer Eric Montross pounded the Jayhawks from inside and Tar Heel guard Donald Williams shot lights out from the outside. It was too much for the Hawks to handle and ended in a 78-68 loss.

But KU had its chances. With 2:48 left, KU was down by three when Walters came back into the game. He was fresh and ready, but he suffered a nightmare end to his KU career. On three possessions, he had two turnovers and a missed jumper, and KU suddenly trailed by 10. It was over.

"The last two years have been the best of my life," Walters said after leaving the floor in tears. "This is a big downer, but it can't take away from what we accomplished. I had a couple of turnovers, and that was a big turning point in the game.

Rex Walters dives over North Carolina forward George Lynch at the semifinal game in New Orleans.

"I can handle losing. A lot of guys would have loved to be in my position."

ROY'S TOUGHEST JOB Williams said the 1992-93 season was his toughest ever, even more so than the probation

Roy Williams and assistant coach Steve Robinson try to get their point across during KU's loss to the Tar Heels at the 1993 Final Four.

years when he first arrived at Kansas.

"It's definitely been the most difficult year I've had in coaching," he said after defeating Indiana in the regional final. "The expectations didn't bother me, but they bothered a couple of our kids. I did a poor job of being able to take the pressure off Adonis and Rex. ... It's been a constant fight every game."

TRY, TRY AGAIN Two trips to the Final Four but no championship. The near misses were difficult for Williams to handle. But after the loss to North Carolina, he vowed that he wouldn't give up in his quest for a national title:

"We've been knocking on the door," he said, "and we're going to keep knocking until we knock it down."

By the Numbers

The statistics, lists and records that appear in this chapter are taken from the KU basketball media guide, which is produced by the KU Sports Information Office. The text was updated through the 1992-93 season.

SEASON BY SEASON SUMMARY

Year	All Games W	L	Conf. W	L	Coach	Captain	Conf. Finish	Post Season
1898-99	7	4	-	-	Naismith	Will Sutton		
1899-00	3	4	-	-	Naismith	Herbert Owens		
1900-01	4	8	-	-	Naismith	Fred Owens		
1901-02	5	7	-	-	Naismith	C.A. Smith		
1902-03	7	8	-	-	Naismith	Joe Alford		
1903-04	5	8	-	-	Naismith	Harry Allen		
1904-05	5	6	-	-	Naismith	C.J. Bliss, I.R. Adams		
1905-06	12	7	-	-	Naismith	M.B. Miller		
1906-07	7	8	-	-	Naismith	M.B. Miller		
1907-08	18	6	6	0	Allen	George McCune	First	
1908-09	25	3	8	2	Allen	Earl Woodard	First	
1909-10	18	1	7	1	Hamilton	Tommy Johnson	First	
1910-11	12	6	9	3	Hamilton	Robert Heizer	First	
1911-12	11	7	6	2	Hamilton	George Stuckey	First	
1912-13	16	6	7	3	Hamilton	Charles Greenlees	Second	
1913-14	17	1	13	1	Hamilton	Ralph Sproull	First-Tie	
1914-15	16	1	13	1	Hamilton	R.A. Dunmire	First	
1915-16	6	12	5	11	Hamilton	Lawrence Cole	Fourth	
1916-17	12	8	9	7	Hamilton	Lawrence S. Nelson	Fourth	
1917-18	10	8	9	8	Hamilton	Rudolph Uhrlaub	Third	
1918-19	7	9	5	9	Hamilton	Kelsey Mathews	Fifth	
1919-20	11	7	9	7	Allen+	Arthur Lonborg	Third	
1920-21	10	8	10	8	Allen	Ernst Uhrlaub	Fourth	
1921-22	16	2	15	1	Allen	George Rody	First-Tie	Helms National Champions
1922-23	17	1	16	0	Allen	Paul Endacott	First	Helms National Champions
1923-24	16	3	15	1	Allen	Charles Black	First	
1924-25	17	1	15	1	Allen	Tusten Ackerman	First	
1925-26	16	2	16	2	Allen	Wilferd Belgard	First	
1926-27	15	2	10	2	Allen	Harold Schmidt	First	
1927-28	9	9	9	9	Allen	James Hill, Glenn Burton	Fourth	
1928-29	3	15	2	8	Allen	Forrest Cox	Fifth-Tie	
1929-30	14	4	7	3	Allen	Russell Thomson	Second	
1930-31	15	3	7	3	Allen	Tom Bishop	First	
1931-32	13	5	7	3	Allen	Ted O'Leary, Lee Page	First	
1932-33	13	4	8	2	Allen	William Johnson	First	
1933-34	16	1	9	1	Allen	Paul Harrington	First	
1934-35	15	5	12	4	Allen	Dick Wells	Second	
1935-36	21	2	10	0	Allen	Ray Ebling	First	Olympic Playoffs
1936-37	15	4	8	2	Allen	Paul Rogers, Ray Noble	First-Tie	
1937-38	18	2	9	1	Allen	Fred Pralle	First	
1938-39	13	7	6	4	Allen	Lyman Corlis	Third	
1939-40	19	6	8	2	Allen	Don Ebling, Dick Harp	First-Tie	NCAA (2nd Place)
1940-41	12	6	7	3	Allen	Howard Engleman, John Kline, Bob Allen	First-Tie	
1941-42	17	5	8	2	Allen	Ralph Miller	First-Tie	NCAA Regional
1942-43	22	6	10	0	Allen	John Buescher	First	
1943-44	17	9	5	5	Allen	Harold McSpadden	Third	
1944-45	12	5	7	3	Allen	Gordon Reynolds, Kirk Scott	Second	
1945-46	19	2	10	0	Allen	*T.P. Hunter	First	
1946-47	16	11	5	5	Allen++	Charlie Black	Third-Tie	
1947-48	9	15	4	8	Allen	Otto Schnellbacher	Sixth-Tie	
1948-49	12	12	3	9	Allen	Bill Sapp	Sixth-Tie	
1949-50	14	11	8	4	Allen	Claude Houchin	First-Tie	
1950-51	16	8	8	4	Allen	Jerry Waugh	Second-Tie	
1951-52	28	3	11	1	Allen	Clyde Lovellette, Bill Lienhard, Bob Kenney, John Keller, Bill Hougland	First	NCAA Champions

Year	All Games W	L	Conf. W	L	Coach	Captain	Conf. Finish	Post Season
1952-53	19	6	10	2	Allen	Dean Kelley	First	NCAA (2nd Place)
1953-54	16	5	10	2	Allen	Al Kelley, B.H. Born	First-Tie	
1954-55	11	10	5	7	Allen	John Anderson	Fifth	
1955-56	14	9	6	6	Allen	Dallas Dobbs	Fifth	
1956-57	24	3	11	1	Harp	Gene Elstun, John Parker	First	NCAA (2nd Place)
1957-58	18	5	8	4	Harp	None Elected	Second-Tie	
1958-59	11	14	8	6	Harp	None Elected	Third-Tie	
1959-60	19	9	10	4	Harp	None Elected	First-Tie	NCAA Regional Finals
1960-61	17	8	10	4	Harp	Bill Bridges, Dee Ketchum	Second-Tie	
1961-62	7	18	3	11	Harp	None Elected	Seventh-Tie	
1962-63	12	13	5	9	Harp	Nolen Ellison	Sixth-Tie	
1963-64	13	12	8	6	Harp	Harry Gibson, Al Correll	Third	
1964-65	17	8	9	5	Owens	David Schichtle	Second	
1965-66	23	4	13	1	Owens	Delvy Lewis, Riney Lochmann	First	NCAA Regional Finals
1966-67	23	4	13	1	Owens	Ron Franz	First	NCAA Regionals
1967-68	22	8	10	4	Owens	Rodger Bohnenstiehl	Second	NIT (2nd Place)
1968-69	20	7	9	5	Owens	Bruce Sloan, JoJo White	Second-Tie	NIT
1969-70	17	9	8	6	Owens	Chester Lawrence	Second	
1970-71	27	3	14	0	Owens	Pierre Russell	First	NCAA (Fourth)
1971-72	11	15	7	7	Owens	Bud Stallworth	Fourth-Tie	
1972-73	8	18	4	10	Owens	Wilson Barrow	Sixth-Tie	
1973-74	23	7	13	1	Owens	Tom Kivisto, Dave Taynor	First	NCAA (Fourth)
1974-75	19	8	11	3	Owens	Danny Knight, Dale Greenlee	First	NCAA Regionals
1975-76	13	13	6	8	Owens	Norman Cook	Fourth-Tie	
1976-77	18	10	8	6	Owens	Ken Koenigs	Fourth	
1977-78	24	5	13	1	Owens	Ken Koenigs, John Douglas	First	NCAA Regionals
1978-79	18	11	8	6	Owens	Paul Mokeski, Brad Sanders	Second-Tie	
1979-80	15	14	7	7	Owens	Randolph Carroll, Mac Stallcup	Third-Tie	
1980-81	24	8	9	5	Owens	Darnell Valentine, Tony Guy	Second-Tie	Big 8 Post-Season Champs NCAA Regional Semifinals
1981-82	13	14	4	10	Owens	Tony Guy, David Magley	Seventh	
1982-83	13	16	4	10	Owens	Jeff Dishman, Mark Summers	Seventh-Tie	
1983-84	22	10	9	5	Brown	Carl Henry, Kelly Knight, Brian Martin	Second	Big 8 Post Season Champs NCAA Regionals
1984-85	26	8	11	3	Brown	Tad Boyle	Second	NCAA Regionals
1985-86	35	4	13	1	Brown	Mark Turgeon, Greg Dreiling	First	Big 8 Post Season Champs NCAA Semifinals
1986-87	25	11	9	5	Brown	Mark Turgeon, Cedric Hunter	Second-Tie	NCAA Regionals
1987-88	27	11	9	5	Brown	Archie Marshall, Danny Manning, Chris Piper	Third	NCAA Champions
1988-89	19	12	6	8	Williams	Milt Newton, Scooter Barry	Sixth	
1989-90	30	5	11	3	Williams	Kevin Pritchard, Rick Calloway, Jeff Gueldner, Freeman West	Second-Tie	NCAA Regionals
1990-91	27	8	10	4	Williams	Terry Brown, Mike Maddox, Mark Randall, Kirk Wagner	First-Tie	NCAA Finals (2nd Place)
1991-92	27	5	11	3	Williams	Alonzo Jamison, Macolm Nash, David Johanning, Lane Czaplinski	First	NCAA Regionals
1992-93	29	7	11	3	Williams	Adonis Jordan, Rex Walters, Eric Pauley	First	NCAA Semifinals

Totals: All Games: 1,515-689 (.687), Conference Games: 755-348 (.684)

+ Schlademan coached season's first game before Allen took over
* Elected posthumously by 1946. Killed in action against the Japanese on Guam, July 21, 1944, while fighting with the Ninth Marines as a first lieutenant.
++ Engleman finished out season as head coach when Allen was ordered to take a rest after 13th game because of head injury.

TEAM RECORDS

POINTS SCORED

Most/Game	150 vs. Kentucky at Lawrence (150-95), Dec. 9, 1989
Most/Conf. Game	127 vs. Iowa State at Lawrence (127-82), Jan. 7, 1989
Most/Game/Both Teams	245 vs. Kentucky at Lawrence (Kansas 150, Kentucky 95), Dec. 9, 1989
Most/Conf. Game/Both Teams	218 vs. Oklahoma at Norman, Okla. (Oklahoma 123, Kansas 95), Jan. 18, 1989
Fewest/Game	5 vs. Kansas City YMCA at Kansas City, Mo., Feb. 3, 1899 (5-16)
	5 vs. Kansas City Athletic Club at Kansas City, Mo., March 27, 1899 (5-19)
Fewest/Conf. Game	9 vs. Kansas State at Manhattan, Feb. 2, 1917 (9-38)
Most/One Half	80 vs. Kentucky (First half) at Lawrence, Dec. 9, 1989
Most/Season	3,223, 1989-90 (92.1 points per game)
Highest Average/Season	92.1 ppg., 1989-90 (3,223 points in 35 games)

FIELD GOALS

Most/Game	52 vs. Kentucky (85 attempts), at Lawrence, Dec. 9, 1989
	52 vs. Elizabeth City State (83 attempts), at Lawrence, Jan. 18, 1990
Most/Season	1,260, in 1985-86
FewestGame	1 vs. Kansas City YMCA at Kansas City, Mo., Feb. 3, 1899
	1 vs. Kansas City Athletic Club at Kansas City, Mo., March 27, 1899
Fewest/Conf. Game	4 vs. Kansas State at Manhattan, Feb. 2, 1917
	4 vs. Missouri at Lawrence, Feb. 28, 1916

FIELD GOAL PERCENTAGE

Highest/Game	75.9% (41-54), vs. Pomona-Pitzer at Lawrence, Dec. 1, 1987
Highest/Season	55.6% (1260-2266) in 1985-86

FREE THROWS

Made/Game	38, 4 times. Most recent: vs. Nebraska at Lincoln, Jan. 8, 1990 (50 attempts)
Made/Conference Game	38, 2 times
Made/Season	618 in 1985-86
Attempted/Season	924 in 1990-91
Fewest Made/Game	0 vs. Warrensburg (Mo.) State at Warrensburg, Feb. 9, 1909
Fewest Made/Conf. Game	1 vs. Kansas State at Manhattan, Feb. 2, 1917

FREE THROW PERCENTAGE

Highest/Game/Conf. Game	100% (11 of 11) vs. Kansas State at Lawrence, Feb. 24, 1968
	100% (11 of 11) vs. Nebraska at Lincoln, Jan. 26, 1977
	100% (11 of 11) vs. Kansas State at Manhattan, Feb. 25, 1984
Highest/Season	73.3% (225-307) in 1948-1949

THREE-POINT FIELD GOALS

Most/Game	11, 7 times. Most recent: vs. North Carolina at New Orleans, April 3, 1993
Most/Season	230 in 1989-90
Attempted/Game	25 vs. Central Missouri State, at Lawrence, Nov. 30, 1991
Attempted/Season	531 in 1989-90

THREE-POINT FIELD GOAL PERCENTAGE

Highest/Game	100% (6-6) vs. Oklahoma State at Stillwater, Feb. 10, 1988
Highest/Conf. Game	100% (6-6) vs. Oklahoma State at Stillwater, Feb. 10, 1988
Highest/Season	43.3% (230-531) in 1989-90

REBOUNDS

Most/Game/Conf. Game	77 vs. Nebraska at Lawrence, Feb. 23, 1957
	77 vs. Missouri at Lawrence, Jan. 5, 1957
Most/Season	1,381 in 1989-90
Highest/Average/Season	51.1 (1,277 in 25 games) in 1960-61

FOULS

Most/Game	39 vs. Notre Dame at Tulsa (NCAA Sub-Regional), March 15, 1975
Fewest/Game	1 vs. Topeka YMCA at Lawrence, Feb. 10, 1899
Fewest/Conf. Game	2 vs. Grinnell at Lawrence, Feb. 24, 1923
	2 vs. Nebraska, at Lincoln, Feb. 12, 1923

STEALS

Most/Game	22 vs. Marquette at Lawrence, Dec. 1, 1990
Most/Season	328 in 1992-93

ASSISTS

Most/Game	36 vs. Kentucky, at Lawrence, Dec. 9, 1989
Most/Season	814 in 1985-86

BLOCKED SHOTS

Most/Game	13 vs. Montana State at Lawrence, Nov. 27, 1976
Most/Season	172 in 1977-78

TURNOVERS

Most/Game	30 vs. Xavier at Lincoln, Neb. (NCAA 1st round), March 18, 1988
Fewest/Game	3 vs. Iowa State, 1966
Most/Season	606 in 1990-91
Fewest/Season	345 in 1967-68

Most Wins/Season	35, (35-4) in 1985-86
Most Wins/Conf. Season	16, (16-2) in 1925-26; (Since 1959) 14, (14-0) in 1970-71
Fewest Wins/Season	3, (3-4) in 1899-1900
Fewest Wins/Conf. Season	2, (2-8) in 1928-29; (Since 1959) 3, (3-11) in 1961-62
Most Losses/Season	18, (7-18) in 1961-62; 18, (8-18) in 1972-73
Most Losses/Conf. Season	11, (3-11) in 1961-62; 11, (5-11) in 1915-16
Fewest Losses/Season	1, six times (most recent, 16-1 in 1933-34)
Fewest Losses/Conf. Season	0, Six times overall; (Since 1959) 14-0 in 1970-71

INDIVIDUAL SCORING

POINTS SCORED

Most/Game	52, Wilt Chamberlain, vs. Northwestern, at Lawrence, 12-3-56
Most/Conf. Game	50, Bud Stallworth, vs. Missouri, at Lawrence, 2-26-72
Most/By a Freshman	35, Danny Manning, vs. Okla. State, at Stillwater, 3-2-85
Most/By a Sophomore	52, Wilt Chamberlain, vs. Northwestern, at Lawrence, 12-3-56
Most/By a Junior	46, John Douglas, vs. Iowa State, at Ames, 2-16-77
	46, Wilt Chamberlain, vs. Nebraska, at Lawrence, 2-8-58
Most/By a Senior	50, Bud Stallworth, vs. Missouri, at Lawrence, 2-26-72
Most in Freshman Debut	21, Norm Cook, vs. Murray State, at Lawrence, 12-1-73
Most in Career Debut	52, Wilt Chamberlain, vs. Northwestern, at Lawrence, 12-3-56
Most/Season	942, Danny Manning, 1987-88 (38 games)
Most/By a Freshman	496, Danny Manning, 1984-85 (34 games)
Most/By a Sophomore	800, Wilt Chamberlain, 1956-57 (27 games)
Most/By a Junior	860, Danny Manning, 1986-87 (36 games)
Most/By a Senior	942, Danny Manning, 1987-88 (38 games)
Most/Conference Season	389, Bud Stallworth, 1971-72 (14 games)
Highest Average/Season	30.1, Wilt Chamberlain, 1957-58 (633 points, 21 games)
Highest Average/Conf. Season	28.3, Wilt Chamberlain, 1957-58 (11 games)
Most/Career	2,951, Danny Manning, 1985-86-87-88 (147 games)
Most/Conference Career	942, Danny Manning, 1985-86-87-88 (56 games)
Highest Average/Career	29.9, Wilt Chamberlain, 1957-58
Highest Average/Conf. Career	26.5, Wilt Chamberlain, 1957-58
Most/2-year Career	1,433, Wilt Chamberlain, 1957-58
Most/3-year Career	1,888, Clyde Lovellette, 1950-51-52

SINGLE GAME SCORING

Player, Date, Opponent	Class	FGM	FTM	Pts.
1. Wilt Chamberlain, 12-3-56 vs. Northwestern	So.	20	12	52
2. Bud Stallworth, 2-26-72 vs. Missouri	Sr.	19	12	50
3. John Douglas, 2-16-77 vs. Iowa State	Jr.	19	8	46
Wilt Chamberlain, 2-8-58 vs. Nebraska	Jr.	14	18	46
5. Wilt Chamberlain, 12-30-57 vs. Colorado	So.	18	9	45
6. Clyde Lovellette, 3-22-52 vs. St. Louis	Sr.	16	12	44
B.H. Born, 3-2-53 vs. Colorado	Jr.	16	12	44
8. Danny Manning, 3-15-87 vs. S.W. Missouri State	Jr.	16	10	42
Clyde Lovellette, 12-14-51 vs. Southern Methodist	Sr.	18	6	42
Walter Wesley, 12-12-65 vs. Loyola of Chicago	Jr.	19	4	42
Terry Brown, 1-5-91 vs. N.C. State	Sr.	14	3	42

SINGLE CONFERENCE GAME SCORING

Player, Date, Opponent	Class	FGM	FTM	Pts.
1. Bud Stallworth, 2-26-72 vs. Missouri	Sr.	19	12	50
2. John Douglas, 2-16-77 vs. Iowa State	Jr.	19	8	46
Wilt Chamberlain, 2-8-58 vs. Nebraska	Jr.	14	18	46
4. B.H. Born, 3-2-53 vs. Colorado	Jr.	16	12	44
5. Clyde Lovellette, 3-10-52 vs. Colorado	Sr.	18	5	41
6. Wilt Chamberlain, 3-9-57 vs. Colorado	Jr.	14	12	40

SINGLE SEASON SCORING

Player, Year	G	FGM	FTM	Pts.	Avg.
1. Danny Manning, 1988	38	381	171	942	24.8
2. Danny Manning, 1987	36	347	165	860	23.9
3. Wilt Chamberlain, 1957	27	275	250	800	29.6
4. Clyde Lovellette, 1952	28	315	165	795	28.4
5. Dave Robisch, 1970	26	250	189	689	26.5
6. Bud Stallworth, 1972	26	277	105	659	25.3
7. Danny Manning, 1986	39	279	95	653	16.7
8. Wilt Chamberlain, 1958	21	228	177	633	30.1
9. Ron Kellogg, 1986	39	244	134	622	15.9
10. Wayne Hightower, 1960	28	209	193	611	21.8

INDIVIDUAL RECORDS

FIELD GOALS

Most/Game	20, Wilt Chamberlain, vs. Northwestern, at Lawrence, 12-3-56
Most/Conf. Game	19, Bud Stallworth, vs. Missouri, at Lawrence, 2-26-72 (38 attempts)
	19, John Douglas, vs. Iowa State, at Ames, 2-16-77 (30 attempts)
Most/Season	347, Danny Manning, 1986-87 (562 attempts, 36 games)
Most/Conf. Season	162, Bud Stallworth, 1971-72 (342 attempts, 14 games)
Highest Pct./Season	64.6% (201-311), Mark Randall, 1988-89 (31 games)
Highest Pct./Conf. Season	76.3% (67-91), Cedric Hunter, 1984-85 (14 games)
Most/Career	1,216, Danny Manning, 1985-88
Most/Conf. Career	504, Danny Manning, 1985-88 (56 games)

FREE THROWS

Most/Game	*22, Verne Long, vs. K.C. Athletic Club, at Kansas City, 2-16-11
Most/Conf. Game	18, Wilt Chamberlain, vs. Nebraska, at Lawrence, 2-8-58 (23 attempts)
Most Consecutive Made /Multiple Games	33, Calvin Thompson, 1983-84
Most/Season	250, Wilt Chamberlain, 1956-57 (399 attempts, 27 games)
Most/Conf Season	103, Wilt Chamberlain, 1956-57 (174 attempts, 12 games)
Highest Pct./Season (Min. 50 attempts)	90.0% (45-50), Allen Correll, 1963-64
Highest Pct./Conf.	91.4% (32-35), Calvin Thompson, 1984-85
Most/Career	541, Darnell Valentine, 1978-81
Most/Conf. Career	243, Dave Robisch, 1969-71
Highest Pct./Career (Min. 200 attempts)	84.9% (225-265), Rex Walters, 1992-93
Highest Pct./Conf. Career	86%, Dale Greenlee, 1973-75
	* Shot all of team's free throws

THREE-POINT FIELD GOALS

Most/Game	11, Terry Brown, vs. N.C. State, at Lawrence, 1-5-91 (17 attempts)
Most Attempted/Game	17, Terry Brown, vs. N.C. State, at Lawrence, 1-5-91
Highest Pct.	100.0% (6-6),Rex Walters, vs. Ball State, 3-18-93
Most/Season	111, Terry Brown, 1990-91 (277 attempts, 35 games)
Most Attempted/Season	277, Terry Brown, 1990-91
Highest Pct./Season	48.6% (69-142), Jeff Gueldner, 1989-90
Most/Career	200, Terry Brown, 1990-91
Most Attempted/Career	485, Terry Brown, 1990-91

REBOUNDS

Most/Game	36, Wilt Chamberlain, vs. Iowa State, at Lawrence, 2-15-58
Most/Conf. Game	36, Wilt Chamberlain, vs. Iowa State, at Lawrence, 2-15-58
Most/Season	510, Wilt Chamberlain, 1956-57 (27 games)
Most/Conf. Season	211, Bill Bridges, 1958-59 (14 games)
Highest Average/Season	18.9, Wilt Chamberlain, 1956-57 (510 rebounds/27 games)
Most/Career	1,187, Danny Manning, 1985-88 (147 games)
Most/Conf. Career	580, Bill Bridges, 1959-61

STEALS

Most/Game	8, Alonzo Jamison, vs. Marquette, at Lawrence, 12-1-90
	8, Alonzo Jamison, vs. Pepperdine, at Lawrence, 1-2-92
Most/Conf. Game	7, 3 times. Most recent: Danny Manning, vs. Missouri, at Columbia, 1-23-86
Most/Season	92, Darnell Valentine, 1980-81
Most/Career	334, Darnell Valentine, 1978-81

BLOCKED SHOTS

Most/Game	7, Danny Manning, vs. Texas Tech, 1-20-86; and vs. Missouri, 1-20-87
	7, Paul Mokeski, vs. Farleigh Dickinson, 11-29-78
Most/Conf. Game	7, Danny Manning, vs. Missouri, 1-20-87
Most/Season	73, Danny Manning, 1987-88
Most/Career	200, Danny Manning, 1985-88

FOULS

Most/Season	123, Chris Piper, 1986-87
Most Disqualifications/Season	16, Vernon Vanoy, 1966-67

ASSISTS

Most/Game	18, Tom Kivisto, vs. Nebraska, at Kansas City, Mo., 12-29-73
Most/Conf. Game	11, 6 times
Most/Season	278, Cedric Hunter, 1985-86
Most/Career	684, Cedric Hunter, 1984-87

MINUTES PLAYED

Most/Season	1,336, Danny Manning, 1987-88 (38 games)
Most/Career	4,961, Danny Manning, 1985-188

CAREER SCORING
(At least 1,000 Points)

Player, Years	G	FGM	FTM	Pts.	Avg.
1. Danny Manning, 1985-86-87-88	147	1216	509	2,951	20.1
2. Clyde Lovellette, 1950-51-52	77	774	340	1,888	24.5
3. Darnell Valentine, 1978-79-80-81	118	640	541	1,821	15.4
4. Dave Robisch, 1969-70-71	83	646	462	1,754	21.1
5. Kevin Pritchard, 1987-88-89-90	139	610	318	1,692	12.2
6. Mark Randall, 1987, 1989-90-91	132	643	340	1,627	12.1
7. Calvin Thompson, 1983-84-85-86	131	630	288	1,548	11.8
8. Ron Kellogg, 1983-84-85-86	130	607	294	1,508	11.6
9. Bud Stallworth, 1970-71-72	82	631	233	1,495	18.2
10. Tony Guy, 1979-80-81-82	117	562	364	1,488	12.7
11. Wilt Chamberlain, 1957-58	48	503	427	1,433	29.9
12. Adonis Jordan, 1990-91-92-93	137	455	284	1,373	10.0
13. Walter Wesley, 1964-65-66	68	496	323	1,315	19.3
14. Jo Jo White, 1966-67-68	84	536	214	1,286	15.3
15. Greg Dreiling, 1984-85-86	104	474	261	1,209	11.6
16. Milt Newton, 1985, 1987-88-89	128	442	182	1,166	9.1
17. Rick Suttle, 1973-74-75	83	487	182	1,156	13.9
18. Wayne Hightower, 1960-61	53	401	326	1,128	21.3
19. Charles Black, 1942-43, 1946-47	87	412	258	1,082	12.4
20. Rex Walters, 1992-93	68	344	225	1,064	15.6
21. Kelly Knight, 1980, 1982-83-84	101	438	181	1,057	10.5
22. Nolen Ellison, 1961-62-63	75	387	271	1,045	13.9
23. Carl Henry, 1983-84	61	405	234	1,044	17.1
24. Jerry Gardner, 1960-61-62	78	405	220	1,030	13.2
25. Bill Bridges, 1959-60-61	78	375	278	1,028	13.2
26. Cedric Hunter, 1984-85-86-87	119	416	189	1,022	8.7
David Magley, 1979-80-81-82	113	418	185	1,022	9.0
27. Rodger Bohnenstiehl, 1966-67-68	82	397	212	1,006	12.3
28. Norman Cook, 1974-75-76	83	414	176	1,004	12.1

CAREER REBOUNDING

Player, Year	G	Reb.	Avg.
1. Danny Manning, 1985-86-87-88	147	1,187	8.1
2. Bill Bridges, 1959-60-61	78	1,081	13.9
3. Wilt Chamberlain, 1957-58	48	877	18.3
4. Dave Robisch, 1969-70-71	83	815	9.8
5. Clyde Lovellette, 1950-51-52	77	813	10.6
6. Mark Randall, 1987, 89-90-91	132	723	5.4
7. Paul Mokeski, 1976-77-78-79	89	680	7.6
8. Greg Dreiling, 1984-85-86	104	650	6.3
9. Roger Brown, 1969-70-71	79	640	8.1
10. Norman Cook, 1974-75-76	83	624	7.5
11. Pierre Russell, 1969-70-71	83	607	7.3
12. Kelly Knight, 1980, 82-83-84	101	601	5.9
13. David Magley, 1979-80-81-82	113	596	5.3
14. Ken Koenigs, 1975-76-77-78	96	585	6.1
15. Wayne Hightower, 1960-61	53	573	10.8
16. Rick Suttle, 1973-74-75	83	569	6.9
17. Gene Elstun, 1955-56-57	70	566	8.1
18. Walter Wesley, 1964-65-66	68	565	8.3
19. Lew Johnson, 1955-56-57	70	561	8.0
Ron Loneski, 1957-58-59	63	561	8.9

SINGLE-GAME REBOUNDING

Player, Year, Opponent	Reb.
1. Wilt Chamberlain, 1958 vs. Iowa State	36
2. Wilt Chamberlain, 1957 vs. Northwestern	31
3. Bill Bridges, 1960 vs. Northwestern	30
4. Wilt Chamberlain, 1957 vs. Washington	28
5. Wilt Chamberlain, 1958 vs. Missouri	27
6. Dave Robisch, 1970 vs. Iowa State	26
7. Lew Johnson, 1955 vs. Oklahoma	24
Wilt Chamberlain, 1957 vs. Wisconson	24
Wilt Chamberlain, 1957 vs. Iowa State	24
Wilt Chamberlain, 1957 vs. Iowa State	24
Bill Bridges, 1959 vs. Nebraska	24
Bill Bridges, 1960 vs. Nebraska	24
13. Wilt Chamberlain, 1958 vs. Washington	22
Wilt Chamberlain, 1957 vs. Marquette	22
Wilt Chamberlain, 1957 vs. Missouri	22
Wilt Chamberlain, 1957 vs. Oklahoma	22
Wilt Chamberlain, 1957 vs. So. Methodist	22
Clyde Lovellette, 1952 vs. Colorado	22

SINGLE-SEASON REBOUNDING
(by total rebounds)

Player, Year	G	Reb.	Avg.
1. Wilt Chamberlain, 1957	27	510	18.9
2. Clyde Lovellette, 1952	31	410	13.2
3. Bill Bridges, 1960	28	385	13.8
4. Wilt Chamberlain, 1958	21	367	17.5
5. Bill Bridges, 1961	25	353	14.1
6. Bill Bridges, 1959	25	343	13.7
7. Danny Manning, 1987	36	342	9.6
Danny Manning, 1988	38	342	9.0
9. Roger Brown, 1971	29	322	11.1
10. Dave Robisch, 1970	26	314	12.1
11. Dave Robisch, 1971	30	302	10.1
12. Wayne Hightower, 1961	25	291	11.6
13. Wayne Hightower, 1960	28	282	10.1
14. B.H. Born, 1953	25	280	11.2
15. Greg Dreiling, 1986	39	262	6.7
16. Danny Manning, 1985	34	258	7.6
17. Pierre Russell, 1970	26	251	9.7
18. Walter Wesley, 1966	27	250	9.3
19. Danny Manning, 1986	39	245	6.3
20. Paul Mokeski, 1979	29	242	8.3
21. Ron Loneski, 1959	24	238	9.9
22. Paul Mokeski, 1978	28	237	8.5
23. Greg Dreiling, 1985	34	235	6.9
24. Pierre Russell, 1971	30	234	7.8
25. Lew Johnson, 1956	23	230	10.0
Lew Johnson, 1955	21	230	11.0
Herb Nobles, 1977	28	230	8.2
28. David Magley, 1982	27	227	8.4
29. Kelly Knight, 1984	32	226	7.0
30. Alonzo Jamison, 1991	35	225	6.4
Rick Suttle, 1973	26	225	8.7
32. Norman Cook, 1975	27	222	8.2
33. Walter Wesley, 2965	25	220	8.8
34. Mark Randall, 1991	35	216	6.2
Mark Randall, 1990	35	216	6.2
36. Danny Knight, 1974	30	213	7.1
37. Clyde Lovellette, 1951	24	211	8.8
38. Kelly Knight, 1983	29	210	7.2
39. Art Housey, 1981	32	208	6.5
Ron Loneski, 1958	23	208	9.0
Al Lopes, 1966	27	208	7.7
Mark Randall, 1989	31	208	6.7
43. Norman Cook, 1976	26	206	7.9

SEASON REBOUND AVERAGE

	Player, Years	Avg.
1.	Wilt Chamberlain, 1956-57	18.9
2.	Wilt Chamberlain, 1957-58	17.5
3.	Bill Bridges, 1960-61	14.1
4.	Bill Bridges, 1959-60	13.8
5.	Bill Bridges, 1958-59	13.7
6.	Clyde Lovellette, 1951-52	13.2
7.	Dave Robisch, 1969-70	12.1
8.	Wayne Hightower, 1960-61	11.6
9.	B.H. Born, 1952-53	11.2
10.	Roger Brown, 1970-71	11.1

CAREER REBOUND AVERAGE

	Player, Years	Avg.
1.	Wilt Chamberlain, 1957-58	18.3
2.	Bill Bridges, 1959-61	13.9
3.	Wayne Hightower, 1960-61	10.8
4.	Clyde Lovellette, 1950-52	10.6
5.	Dave Robisch, 1969-71	9.8
6.	Ron Loneski, 1957-59	8.9
7.	Walter Wesley, 1964-66	8.3
8.	Roger Brown, 1969-71	8.1
	Gene Elstun, 1955-57	8.1
	Danny Manning, 1985-88	8.1

SINGLE-GAME ASSISTS (Beginning 1973-74)

	Player, Date, Opponent	Assists
1.	Tom Kivisto, 12-29-73 vs. Nebraska	18
2.	Cedric Hunter, 3-8-86 vs. Oklahoma	16
3.	Cedric Hunter, 12-1-85 vs. Duke	14
4.	Cedric Hunter, 1-4-86 vs. Memphis State	12
	Adonis Jordan, 1-5-91 vs. N.C. State	12
6.	Tom Kivisto, 2-18-74 vs. Oklahoma	11
	Darnell Valentine, 2-2-79 vs. Oklahoma State	11
	Darnell Valentine, 2-27-79 vs. Iowa State	11
	Darnell Valentine, 2-7-80 vs. Iona	11
	Darnell Valentine, 2-26-80 vs. Colorado	11
	Tony Guy, 11-29-80 vs. Nevada-Reno	11
	Darnell Valentine, 12-1-80 vs. Pepperdine	11
	Cedric Hunter, 2-20-85 vs. Kansas State	11
	Cedric Hunter, 12-14-85 vs. Kentucky	11
	Cedric Hunter, 1-23-86 vs. Missouri	11
	Cedric Hunter, 3-13-86 vs. N. Carolina A&T	11
	Scooter Barry, 12-30-88 vs. SW Missouri State	11
	Steve Woodberry, 1-10-91 vs. Md.-Balt. Co.	11
	Adonis Jordan, 3-18-93 vs. Ball State	11

SEASON ASSISTS (Beginning 1974-75)

	Player, Years	Assists
1.	Cedric Hunter, 1985-86	278
2.	Cedric Hunter, 1986-87	209
3.	Kevin Pritchard, 1989-90	177
4.	Darnell Valentine, 1978-79	170
5.	Darnell Valentine, 1980-81	168
6.	Adonis Jordan, 1992-93	163
7.	Scooter Barry, 1988-89	155
8.	Adonis Jordan, 1990-91	154
	Rex Walters, 1992-93	154
10.	Cedric Hunter, 1984-85	145

CAREER ASSISTS (Beginning 1974-75)

	Player, Years	Assists
1.	Cedric Hunter, 1984-87	684
2.	Darnell Valentine, 1978-81	609
3.	Adonis Jordan, 1990-93	568
4.	Kevin Pritchard, 1987-90	499
5.	Mark Turgeon, 1984-87	437
6.	Danning Manning, 1985-88	342
7.	Tony Guy, 1979-82	327
8.	Calvin Thompson, 1983-86	321
9.	Rex Walters, 1992-93	278
10.	Ron Kellogg, 1983-86	272

SINGLE GAME BLOCKED SHOTS (Beginning 1976-77)

	Player, Date, Opponent	Shots
1.	Paul Mokeski, 11-29-78 vs. Fairleigh Dickinson	7
	Danny Manning, 12-20-86 vs. Texas Tech	7
	Danny Manning, 1-20-87 vs. Missouri	7
4.	Herb Nobles, 2-5-77 vs. Oklahoma	6
	Paul Mokeski, 1-13-79 vs. Oklahoma State	6
	Greg Dreiling, 12-17-83 vs. Florida Southern	6
	Danny Manning, 4-2-88 vs. Duke	6
8.	Donnie Von Moore (Three Times, 1976-77)	5
	Johnny Crawford (Five Times, 1978-81)	5
	Chester Giles, 1-5-80 vs. Wisconsin-Oshkosh	5
	Brian Martin, 12-11-82 vs. Southern Methodist	5
	Kelly Knight, 3-11-83 vs. Oklahoma State	5
	Greg Dreiling (Two Times, 1984-86)	5
	Danny Manning (Three Times, 1985-88)	5
	Greg Ostertag, 2-27-93 vs. Colorado	5

SEASON BLOCKED SHOTS (Beginning 1976-77)

	Player, Years	Shots
1.	Danny Manning, 1987-88	73
2.	John Crawford, 1978-79	57
3.	Greg Dreiling, 1984-85	55
4.	Paul Mokeski, 1977-78	54
5.	Donnie Von Moore, 1977-78	53
6.	John Crawford, 1980-81	52
7.	Donnie Von Moore, 1976-77	51
	Paul Mokeski, 1978-79	51
9.	Herb Nobles, 1976-77	48
10.	Danny Manning, 1986-87	47

CAREER BLOCKED SHOTS (Beginning 1976-77)

	Player, Years	Shots
1.	Danny Manning, 1985-88	200
2.	John Crawford, 1978-81	155
3.	Donnie Von Moore, 1975, 1977-78	147
4.	Greg Dreiling, 1984-86	138
5.	Paul Mokeski, 1976-79	136
6.	Herb Nobles, 1975-77	86
7.	Brian Martin, 1982-84	83
8.	Greg Ostertag, 1992-?	70
9.	Kelly Knight, 1980, 1982-84	65
10.	Ken Koenigs, 1975-78	58

SINGLE GAME STEALS (Beginning 1975-76)

	Player, Date, Opponent	Steals
1.	Alonzo Jamison, 12-1-90 vs. Marquette	8
	Alonzo Jamison, 1-2-92 vs. Pepperdine	8
3.	Darnell Valentine, 11-30-77 vs. Fordham	7
	Tony Guy, 2-17-79 vs. Kansas State	7
	Darnell Valentine, 2-7-81 vs. Oklahoma	7
	Danny Manning, 1-23-86 vs. Missouri	7
	Kevin Pritchard, 12-1-87 vs. Pomona-Pitzer	7
	Adonis Jordan, 12-21-92 vs. N.C. State	7
9.	John Douglas, 12-2-77 vs. Southern Methodist	6
	Darnell Valentine (Eight Times, 1978-81)	6
	Tony Guy, 1-9-80 vs. Missouri	6
	Danny Manning (Six Times, 1985-88)	6
	Mark Randall, 1-9-89 vs. Southern Methodist	6
	Alonzo Jamison, 1-19-91 vs. Missouri	6
	Alonzo Jamison, 2-19-92 vs. Nebraska	6

SEASON STEALS (Beginning 1976-77)

	Player, Years	Steals
1.	Darnell Valentine, 1980-81	92
2.	Darnell Valentine, 1978-79	91
3.	Alonzo Jamison, 1991-92	83
4.	Alonzo Jamison, 1990-91	80
	Danny Manning, 1985-86	80
	Darnell Valentine, 1977-78	80
7.	Darnell Valentine, 1979-80	73
8.	Danny Manning, 1987-88	70
	Adonis Jordan, 1992-93	70
10.	Cedric Hunter, 1985-86	61

CAREER STEALS (Beginning 1976-77)

Player, Years	Steals
1. Darnell Valentine, 1978-81	334
2. Danny Manning, 1985-88	270
3. Kevin Pritchard, 1987-90	200
4. Adonis Jordan, 1990-93	181
5. Alonzo Jamison, 1990-92	175
6. Tony Guy, 1979-82	161
7. Cedric Hunter, 1984-87	157
8. Clint Johnson, 1975-78	127
9. Mark Randall, 1987, 1989-91	108
10. David Magley, 1979-82	99

SEASON FIELD GOALS MADE

Player, Year	FGM
1. Danny Manning, 1987-88	381
2. Danny Manning, 1986-87	347
3. Clyde Lovellette, 1951-52	315
4. Danny Manning, 1985-86	279
5. Bud Stallworth, 1971-72	277
6. Wilt Chamberlain, 1956-67	275
7. Ron Kellogg, 1984-85	250
Dave Robisch, 1969-70	250
9. Clyde Lovellette, 1950-51	245
10. Ron Kellogg, 1985-86	244

SEASON FIELD GOALS ATTEMPTED

Player, Years	FGA
1. Clyde Lovellette, 1951-52	660
2. Danny Manning, 1987-88	653
3. Bud Stallworth, 1971-72	620
4. Wilt Chamberlain, 1956-57	588
5. Danny Manning, 1986-87	562
6. Clyde Lovellette, 1950-51	554
7. Dave Robisch, 1969-70	526
8. Wayne Hightower, 1959-60	512
9. Dave Robisch, 1970-71	511
10. Wilt Chamberlain, 1957-58	482

SEASON FIELD GOAL PERCENTAGE

(Minimum 175 attempts)

Player, Years	FGM	FGA	FG%
1. Mark Randall, 1988-89	201	311	64.6
2. Mark Randall, 1990-91	205	319	64.3
3. Richard Scott, 1991-92	138	216	63.9
4. Danny Manning, 1986-87	347	562	61.7
5. Freeman West, 1988-89	111	181	61.3
6. Richard Scott, 1992-93	155	255	60.8
7. Ken Koenigs, 1977-78	123	204	60.3
8. Mark Randall, 1989-90	183	305	60.0
Greg Dreiling, 1985-86	180	300	60.0
Danny Manning, 1985-86	279	465	60.0

CAREER FIELD GOALS MADE

Player, Years	FGM
1. Danny Manning, 1985-88	1,216
2. Clyde Lovellette, 1950-52	774
3. Dave Robisch, 1969-71	646
4. Mark Randall, 1987, 1989-91	643
5. Darnell Valentine, 1978-81	640
6. Bud Stallworth, 1970-72	631
7. Calvin Thompson, 1983-86	630
8. Kevin Pritchard, 1987-90	610
9. Ron Kellogg, 1983-86	607
10. Tony Guy, 1979-82	562

CAREER FIELD GOALS ATTEMPTED

Player, Years	FGA
1. Danny Manning, 1985-88	2,049
2. Clyde Lovellette, 1950-52	1,713
3. Bud Stallworth, 1970-72	1,413
4. Dave Robisch, 1969-71	1,410
5. Darnell Valentine, 1978-81	1,344
6. Jo Jo White, 1966-67	1,276
7. Kevin Pritchard, 1987-90	1,233
8. Calvin Thompson, 1983-86	1,180
9. Tony Guy, 1979-82	1,172
10. Ron Kellogg, 1983-86	1,142

CAREER FIELD GOAL PERCENTAGE (Min. 500 attempts)

Player, Years	FGM	FGA	FG%
1. Mark Randall, 1987, 1989-91	643	1,037	62.0
2. Danning Manning, 1985-88	1,216	2,049	59.3
3. Alonzo Jamison, 1990-92	296	510	58.0
4. Greg Dreiling, 1984-86	474	828	57.2
5. Kelly Knight, 1980, 1982-84	438	782	56.0
6. Mike Maddox, 1988-91	400	723	55.3
7. Carl Henry, 1983-84	405	736	55.0
8. Cedric Hunter, 1984-87	416	778	53.4
Calvin Thompson, 1983-86	630	1,180	53.4
10. Ron Kellogg, 1983-86	607	1,142	53.2
Ken Koenigs, 1975-78	356	669	53.2

SEASON FREE THROWS MADE

Player, Year	FTM
1. Wilt Chamberlain, 1956-57	250
2. Wayne Hightower, 1959-60	193
3. Dave Robisch, 1969-70	189
4. Clyde Lovellette, 1951-52	182
5. Wilt Chamberlain, 1957-58	177
6. Danny Manning, 1987-88	171
7. Danny Manning, 1986-87	165
8. Walter Wesley, 1965-66	159
9. Darnell Valentine, 1979-80	153
10. B.H. Born, 1952-53	148

CAREER FREE THROWS MADE

Player, Years	FTM
1. Darnell Valentine, 1978-81	541
2. Danny Manning, 1985-88	509
3. Dave Robisch, 1969-71	462
4. Wilt Chamberlain, 1957-58	427
5. Tony Guy, 1979-82	364
6. Clyde Lovellette, 1950-52	357
7. Mark Randall, 1987, 89-91	340
8. Wayne Hightower, 1960-61	326
9. Walter Wesley, 1964-66	323
10. Kevin Pritchard, 1987-90	318

SEASON FREE THROWS ATTEMPTED

Player, Years	FTA
1. Wilt Chamberlain, 1956-57	399
2. Wilt Chamberlain, 1957-58	292
3. Wayne Hightower, 1959-60	285
4. Walter Wesley, 1965-66	262
5. Dave Robisch, 1969-70	254
6. Clyde Lovellette, 1951-52	250
7. B.H. Born, 1952-53	243
8. Dave Robisch, 1970-71	233
Danny Manning, 1987-88	233
10. Danny Manning, 1986-87	226

CAREER FREE THROWS ATTEMPTED

Player, Years	FTA
1. Darnell Valentine, 1978-81	754
2. Wilt Chamberlain, 1957-58	691
3. Danny Manning, 1985-88	688
4. Dave Robisch, 1969-71	677
5. Walter Wesley, 1964-66	544
6. Clyde Lovellette, 1950-52	520
7. Tony Guy, 1979-82	492
8. Wayne Hightower, 1960-61	484
9. B.H. Born, 1952-54	472
10. Bill Bridges, 1959-61	426

SEASON FREE-THROW PERCENTAGE (Min. 45 att.)

Player, Years	FTM	FTA	FT%
1. Allen Correll, 1963-64	45	50	90.0
2. Dale Greenlee, 1973-74	43	48	89.6
3. Steve Woodberry, 1992-93	87	99	87.9
4. Rex Walters, 1992-93	110	126	87.3
5. Al Kelley, 1953-54	75	87	86.2
6. Calvin Thompson, 1983-84	67	78	85.8
7. Ken Koenigs, 1976-77	72	85	84.7
8. Dave Magley, 1980-81	55	65	84.6
9. Ron Kellogg, 1984-85	97	115	84.3
Ron Kellogg, 1985-86	134	159	84.3

CAREER FREE THROW PERCENTAGE (Min. 100 attempts)

Player, Years	FTM	FTA	FT%
1. Rex Walters, 1992-93	225	265	84.9
2. Allen Correll, 1960-61, 63-64	151	181	83.4
3. Dale Greenlee, 1973-75	99	119	83.2
4. Ron Kellogg, 1983-86	294	355	82.8
5. Calvin Thompson, 1983-86	288	351	82.0
6. Dee Ketchum, 1959-61	103	130	79.2
7. Bob Kenney, 1950-52	163	206	79.1
David Magley, 1979-82	185	234	79.1
9. Jerry Gardner, 1960-62	220	283	77.7
10.Ken Koenigs, 1975-78	230	297	77.4
Kevin Pritchard, 1987-90	318	411	77.4

SEASON THREE-POINT FIELD GOALS MADE

Player, Year	3PTM
1. Terry Brown, 1990-91	111
2. Terry Brown, 1989-90	89
3. Rex Walters, 1992-93	83
4. Jeff Gueldner, 1989-90	69
5. Rex Walters, 1991-92	68
6. Milt Newton, 1988-89	65
Adonis Jordan, 1992-93	65
8. Kevin Pritchard, 1988-89	55
9. Adonis Jordan, 1991-92	53
10.Adonis Jordan, 1990-91	47

SEASON THREE-POINT FIELD GOAL ATTEMPTS

Player, Years	3PTA
1. Terry Brown, 1990-91	277
2. Terry Brown, 1989-90	208
3. Rex Walters, 1992-93	193
4. Rex Walters, 1991-92	168
5. Adonis Jordan, 1992-93	152
6. Milt Newton, 1988-89	143
7. Jeff Gueldner, 1989-90	142
8. Adonis Jordan, 1991-92	130
9. Kevin Pritchard, 1988-89	129
10.Adonis Jordan, 1990-91	115

SEASON THREE-POINT FIELD GOAL PERCENTAGE
(Min. 40 field goal attempts)

Player, Year	3PTM-A	Pct.
1. Jeff Gueldner, 1989-90	69-142	48.6
2. Milt Newton, 1988-89	65-143	45.5
3. Milt Newton, 1987-88	29-64	45.3
4. Steve Woodberry, 1992-93	25-58	43.1
5. Rex Walters, 1992-93	83-193	43.0
6. Adonis Jordan, 1992-93	65-152	42.8
Terry Brown, 1989-90	89-208	42.8
8. Kevin Pritchard, 1988-89	55-128	42.6
9. Kevin Pritchard, 1989-90	46-108	42.6
10.Patrick Richey, 1990-91	17-41	41.5

CAREER THREE-POINT FIELD GOALS MADE

Player, Year	3PTM
1. Terry Brown, 1990-91	200
2. Adonis Jordan, 1990-93	179
3. Kevin Pritchard, 1987-90	154
4. Rex Walters, 1992-93	151
5. Milt Newton, 1985, 1987-89	100

CAREER THREE-POINT FIELD GOAL PERCENTAGE
(Min. 100 Field Goal Attempts)

Player, Year	3PTM-A	Pct.
1. Milt Newton, 1985, 1987-89	100-224	44.6
2. Jeff Gueldner, 1987-90	90-205	43.9
3. Rex Walters, 1992-93	151-361	41.8
4. Terry Brown, 1990-91	200-485	41.2
5. Adonis Jordan, 1990-93	179-437	41.0

CAREER THREE-POINT FIELD GOAL ATTEMPTS

Player, Year	3PTA
1. Terry Brown, 1990-91	485
2. Adonis Jordan, 1990-Present	433
3. Kevin Pritchard, 1987-90	379
4. Rex Walters, 1992-Present	361
5. Milt Newton, 1985, 1987-89	224

ATTENDANCE IN ALLEN FIELDHOUSE
(since 1964-65)

Year	Attendance	Games	Average	Season Record	Home Record
1964-65	84.642	10	8,464	17-8	7-3
1965-66	124,300	10	12,430	23-4	10-0
1966-67	171,750	13	13,208	23-4	12-1
1967-68	171,924	12	14,327	22-8	9-3
1968-69	167,949	12	13,996	20-7	10-2
1969-70	150,972	13	11,613	17-9	13-0
1970-71	187,750	14	13,411	27-3	14-0
1971-72	175,050	14	12,504	11-15	11-3
1972-73	160,200	14	11,442	8-18	7-7
1973-74	158,550	13	12,196	23-7	12-1
1974-75	166,025	13	12,771	19-8	11-2
1975-76	146,220	14	10,444	13-13	8-6
1976-77	145,488	14	10,392	18-10	12-2
1977-78	182,250	15	12,150	24-5	14-1
1978-79	195,980	14	13,999	18-11	11-2
1979-80	186,703	15	12,447	15-14	11-3
1980-81	198,329	15	13,222	24-8	14-1
1981-82	152,293	16	9,518	13-14	12-4
1982-83	132,251	14	9,447	13-16	8-6
1983-84	185,400	16	11,587	22-10	14-2
1984-85	212,828	16	13,301	26-8	16-0
1985-86	213,034	15	14,202	35-4	15-0
1986-87	233,800	15	15,587	25-11	15-0
1987-88	216,650	14	15,475	27-11	11-3
1988-89	202,488	14	14,463	19-12	10-4
1989-90	242,225	16	15,139	30-5	15-1
1990-91	230,600	15	15,373	27-8	15-0
1991-92	219,550	14	15,682	27-5	13-1
1992-93	235,000	15	15,667	29-7	13-2
Total	5,250,201	405	12,963	615-275	13-2

OPPONENT RECORDS

SINGLE GAME SCORING

Player, School, Year	Pts.	Site	Kansas W/L
1. Lindsey Hunter, Jackson State, 1992-93	48	at Honolulu, Hawaii	W, 93-85
2. Mike Wroblewski, Kansas State, 1961-62	46	at Lawrence, Kan.	L, 72-91
3. Oscar Robertson, Cincinnati, 1959-60	43	at Manhattan, Kan.	L, 71-82
Anthony Peeler, Missouri, 1991-92	43	at Lawrence, Kan.	W, 97-89
5. Chuck Gardner, Colorado 1965-66	39	at Lawrence, Kan.	W, 85-65

Most Points - 48, Lindsey Hunter, Jackson State, Dec. 27, 1992
Most Field Goals - 19, Oscar Robertson, Cincinnati, 1960
Most Field Goals, Conference Game - 17, Mike Wroblewski, Kansas State, 1962
Most Free Throws - 15, Tom Johnson, Missouri, at Columbia, 1968, (18 attempts); Don Tomlinson, Missouri, at Lawrence, 1969, (18 attempts)
Most Rebounds - 27, Bob Nordman, St. Louis, at St. Louis, 1959
Most Rebounds, Conference Game - 22, Chuck Duncan, Iowa State, at Lawrence, 1955
Most Three-Point Field Goals Made - 11, Derrick Miller, Kentucky, at Lawrence, Dec. 9, 1989;
   Lindsey Hunter, Jackson State, at Honolulu Hawaii, Dec. 27, 1992
Most Three-Point Field Goals Attempted - 26, Lindsey Hunter, Jackson State, at Honolulu Hawaii, Dec. 27, 1992
Highest Three-Point Field Goal Percentage (min. 5 attempts) - .714 (5-7), Jeff Moe, Iowa, 1988

Most Points - 123, Oklahoma, at Norman, 1-18-89
Most Points, Conference Opponent - 123, Oklahoma, at Norman, 1-18-89
Most Field Goals - 47, Kentucky, at Lexington, 1970
Most Field Goals, Conference Opponent - 42, Kansas State, at Manhattan, 1979, Oklahoma at Norman, 1-18-89
Most Free Throws - 38, Oklahoma State, at Stillwater, 1972, (43 attempts)
Most Free Throws, Non-Conference Opponent - 37, Oklahoma City,at Lawrence, 1971, (49 attempts)
Most Fouls - 38 - Oklahoma, 1953, (Kansas City)
Most Fouls, Conference Game - 33, Missouri, at Lawrence, 1954, and Nebraska, at Lawrence, 1958
Most Rebounds - 62, St. Louis, at Lawrence, 1968
Most Rebounds, Conference Opponent - 58, Missouri, at Columbia, 1957
Most Three-Point Field Goals Made - 17, Kentucky, at Lawrence, 12-9-89
Most Three-Point Field Goals Attempted - 40, Kentucky, at Lawrence, 12-9-89
Highest Three-Point Field Goal Percentage - .750 (9-12), Kansas State, 1988

Fewest Points - 3, William Jewell, 1899, (19-3)
Fewest Points, Conference Game - 8, Iowa State, 1925, (28-8)
Fewest Field Goals - 1, William Jewell, 1899
Fewest Field Goals, Conference Game - 2, Iowa State, 1925
Fewest Free Throws - 0, Topeka YMCA, 1899
Fewest Free Throws, Conference Game - 1, Drake, 1923; 1 Kansas State, Feb. 22, 1992
Fewest Fouls - 0, Kansas State, 1915

VICTORY MARGINS

	Score	M	Opponent	Season
1.	115-45	(70)	Brown	1988-89
2.	140-72	(68)	Oral Roberts	1992-93
3.	132-65	(67)	Elizabeth City State	1989-90
4.	122-58	(64)	Maryland-Baltimore Co	1991-92
5.	68-8	(60)	Washington (St. Louis)	1912-13
6.	104-47	(57)	Montana State	1976-77
7.	121-65	(56)	Central Missouri State	1977-78
	102-46	(56)	Nebraska	1957-58
	94-38	(56)	Pomona-Pitzer	1987-88
9.	102-47	(55)	Rollins College	1980-81
	150-95	(55)	Kentucky	1989-90
	103-48	(55)	Tennessee-Martin	1989-90

123-95 vs. Oklahoma 1-18-89
115-85 vs. Kentucky 12-6-69
103-84 vs. Oklahoma 1-31-84
103-86 vs. Arkansas 12-6-86
102-77 vs. Duke 2-18-89
100-63 vs. Kentucky 12-23-74
100-81 vs. Iowa 11-28-87
100-78 vs. Oklahoma 2-27-90

	Score	M.	Opponent	Season
1.	48-8	(40)	Nebraska	1899-1900
2.	100-63	(37)	Kentucky	1974-75
3.	41-10	(31)	Missouri	1915-16
4.	115-85	(30)	Kentucky	1969-70
	99-69	(30)	Missouri	1975-76
6.	38-9	(29)	Kansas State	1916-17
7.	68-39	(29)	Kentucky	1950-51
8.	49-21	(28)	Nebraska	1911-12
	97-69	(28)	Oklahoma	1971-72
	123-95	(28)	Oklahoma	1988-89

	Score	M.	Opponent	Season
1.	91-66	(25)	Missouri	1988-89
2.	89-65	(24)	Iowa State	1972-73
	70-46	(24)	Kansas State	1963-64
4.	91-72	(19)	Kansas State	1961-62
	56-37	(19)	Oklahoma State	1961-62
7.	72-55	(17)	Indiana	1972-73
8.	79-63	(16)	Missouri	1972-73
	73-57	(16)	Colorado	1962-63
10.	64-49	(15)	Cincinnati	1962-63

150-95 vs. Kentucky	12-9-89
140-72 vs. Oral Roberts	1-14-93
132-65 vs. Elizabeth City State	1-18-90
127-82 vs. Iowa State	1-7-89
122-58 vs. Maryland-Baltimore Co.	11-23-91
121-65 vs. Central Missouri State	11-28-77
118-75 vs. Iowa State	3-9-90
115-45 vs. Brown	1-3-89
112-76 vs. Missouri	3-9-74
112-61 vs. Pacific Lutheran	12-7-88
111-83 vs. Colorado	2-25-89
111-58 vs. Hawaii Loa	12-28-90
110-73 vs. Nebraska	2-26-66
110-72 vs. Rider	12-12-87
109-76 vs. Southern Mississippi	12-27-91
109-72 vs. Wisconsin-Oshkosh	1-5-80
109-83 vs. Alabama-Birmingham	11-15-89
109-59 vs. Northern Arizona	12-12-88
109-87 vs. Oklahoma	2-23-91
108-71 vs. Marquette	12-1-90
108-62 vs. UMKC	12-12-92
107-71 vs. Southern Methodist	12-2-77
106-71 vs. Murray State	12-5-77
105-94 vs. N.C. State	1-5-91
104-46 vs. Nebraska	2-8-58
104-81 vs. Western Kentucky	12-20-69
104-75 vs. DePaul	12-19-91
104-47 vs. Montana State	11-27-76
103-78 vs. Nebraska	1-25-92
103-71 vs. Murray State	12-1-73
103-48 vs. Tennessee-Martin	12-4-89
103-83 vs. Texas-Pam American	12-29-89
103-71 vs. Colorado	2-21-90
103-51 vs. Rider	12-15-90
103-54 vs. Wichita State	1-6-93
103-56 vs. Rollins	1-30-93
102-51 vs. New Mexico State	12-7-65
102-47 vs. Rollins College	12-30-80
101-77 vs. Oklahoma City	1-16-71
101-69 vs. Texas-San Antonio	12-22-90
101-64 vs. Texas Southern	1-11-84
101-79 vs. Western Carolina	12-4-85
100-66 vs. Howard	3-20-92
100-73 vs. Miami, Fla.	1-10-90
100-64 vs. Colorado	2-5-86
100-66 vs. Missouri	2-11-86
100-52 vs. Xavier	12-3-66
100-87 vs. Nebraska	2-17-70
100-82 vs. Iowa State	1-18-78
100-72 vs. Rice	12-18-54
100-80 vs. Loyola-Chicago	12-3-88
100-67 vs. Iona	12-29-88

OVERTIME/WIN STREAKS

Games	Season/Seasons	Team That Ended Streak
23	1934-35 to 1935-36	Utah State, 42-37, Olympic Playoffs, at Kansas City, Mo.
22	1907-08 to 1908-09	Washington of St. Louis, 28-26, at St. Louis, Mo.
21	1970-71	UCLA, 68-60, NCAA Tournament Semifinals, at Houston, Tx.
21	1913-14 to 1914-15	Kansas State, 21-18, at Lawrence, Ks.
19	1989-90	Missouri, 95-87, at Columbia, Mo.
18	1925-26 to 1926-27	Iowa State, 15-12, at Lawrence, Ks.
16	1950-51 to 1951-52	Kansas State, 81-64, at Manhattan, Ks.
16	1985-86	Duke, 71-67, NCAA Semifinals at Dallas, Tx.
15	1951-52	Peoria Caterpillars, 62-60, Olympic Playoffs, at New York, N.Y.

Games	Season/Seasons	Court	Team That Ended Streak
55*	1983-84 to 1987-88	Allen Fieldhouse	Kansas State, 71-62
33	1950-51 to 1954-55	Hoch Auditorium	Missouri, 76-65
28	1969-70 to 1971-72	Allen Fieldhouse	Kentucky, 79-69
26	1937-38 to 1940-41	Hoch Auditorium	Oklahoma, 45-37
24	1989-90 to 1991-92	Allen Fieldhouse	Louisville, 85-78
21	1965-66 to 1966-67	Allen Fieldhouse	Houston, 66-63 (NCAA Tournament)
20	1921-22 to 1923-24	Robinson Gymnasium	Kansas State, 40-28

* Big Eight Conference record

Number	Date	Opponent	Site	Score	Coach
100	Jan. 15, 1910	Washington (St. Louis)	St. Louis, Mo.	34-13	W.O. Hamilton
200	Jan. 24, 1917	Kansas State	Lawrence	27-19	W.O. Hamilton
300	Feb. 9, 1925	Iowa State	Lawrence	33-18	F.C. Allen
400	Jan. 2, 1933	Stanford	Lawrence	34-28	F.C. Allen
500	Jan. 18, 1939	Missouri	Lawrence	37-32	F.C. Allen
600	Jan. 30, 1945	Kansas State	Lawrence	39-36	F.C. Allen
700	Dec. 29, 1951	Missouri	Kansas City, Mo.	75-65	F.C. Allen
800	Mar. 15, 1957	Southern Methodist	Dallas, Tx.	73-65	Dick Harp
900	Dec. 1, 1964	Arkansas	Fayetteville, Ark.	65-60	Ted Owens
1000	Feb. 3, 1969	Oklahoma State	Lawrence	64-48	Ted Owens
1100	Jan. 25, 1975	Oklahoma State	Lawrence	71-60	Ted Owens
1200	Dec. 1, 1980	Pepperdine	Lawrence	81-67	Ted Owens
1300	Dec. 3, 1985	SIU-Edwardsville	Lawrence	86-71	Larry Brown
1400	Feb. 25, 1989	Colorado	Lawrence	111-83	Roy Williams
1500	Jan. 16, 1993	Louisville	Louisville, Ky.	98-77	Roy Williams

(Based on Percentage)

Year	Record	Coach	Pct.
1909-10	18-1	W.O. Hamilton	.947
1913-14	17-1	W.O. Hamilton	.944
1922-23	17-1	Dr. F.C. Allen	.944
1924-25	17-1	Dr. F.C. Allen	.944
1914-15	16-1	W.O. Hamilton	.941
1933-34	16-1	Dr. F.C. Allen	.941
1935-36	21-2	Dr. F.C. Allen	.913
1945-46	19-2	Dr. F.C. Allen	.905
1951-52	28-3	Dr. F.C. Allen	.903
1970-71	27-3	Ted Owens	.900

Record	Season	Coach
35-4	1985-86	Larry Brown
30-5	1989-90	Roy Williams
29-7	1992-93	Roy Williams
28-3	1951-52	Dr. F.C. Allen
27-3	1970-71	Ted Owens
27-5	1991-92	Roy Williams
27-8	1990-91	Roy Williams
27-11	1987-88	Larry Brown
26-8	1984-85	Larry Brown
25-3	1908-09	Dr. F.C. Allen
25-11	1986-87	Larry Brown

KANSAS NATIONAL CHAMPIONSHIP BOX SCORES

1922 HELMS FOUNDATION CHAMPIONSHIP

Kansas 26, Missouri 8
February, 21, 1922
Columbia, Mo.

Kansas (26)	FG	FT	PF	TP
Frederick, f	0	0	0	0
Rody, f	3	6	1	12
Bowman, f	2	0	4	4
McDonald, f	0	0	0	0
Wulf, c	1	0	2	2
Black, g	1	0	0	2
Endacott, g	3	0	2	6
Totals	10	6	9	26

Missouri (16)	FG	FT	PF	TP
Browning, f	2	0	0	4
Knight, f	2	0	5	4
Vanice, f	0	0	0	0
Bunker, c	0	0	3	0
Bond, g	1	6	1	8
Hays, g	0	0	3	0
Faurot, g	0	0	1	0
Totals	5	6	13	16

Referee-E.C. Quigley, St. Marys
Umpire-Leslie Edmonds, Ottawa

1923 HELMS FOUNDATION CHAMPIONSHIP

Kansas 23, Missouri 20
February 28, 1923
Lawrence, Kan.

Kansas (23)	FG	FT	PT	TP
Ackerman, f	0	7	2	7
Bowman, f	2	0	3	4
Wulf, c	3	0	0	6
Black, g	1	0	1	4
Endacott, g	2	0	2	4
Totals	8	7	8	23

Missouri (20)	FG	FT	PF	TP
Browning, f	1	6	2	8
Wheat, f	5	0	2	10
Bunker, c	1	0	0	2
Faurot, g	0	0	1	0
Vanice, g	0	0	0	0
Hays, g	0	0	3	0
Totals	7	6	9	20

Referee-E.C.Quigley, St. Marys
Umpire-Leslie Edmonds, Ottawa

1952 NCAA CHAMPIONSHIP

Kansas 80, St. John's 63
March 26, 1952 - Seattle, Wash.

Kansas (80)	FG	FT	PF	TP
Kenney	4	4	2	12
Keller	1	0	2	2
Lovellette	12	9	4	33
Lienhard	5	2	4	12
Kelley, D.	2	3	5	7
Hoag	2	5	5	9
Hougland	2	1	2	5
Davenport	0	0	1	0
Heitholt	0	0	0	0
Born	0	0	0	0
Kelley, A.	2	0	0	4
Totals	28	24	25	80

St. John's (63)	FG	FT	PF	TP
McMahon	6	1	4	13
Davis	1	2	4	4
Zawoluk	7	6	5	20
Duckett	2	2	4	6
MacGilvary	3	2	3	8
Walsh	3	0	3	6
McMorrow	1	0	3	2
Sagona	2	0	5	4
Giancontieri	0	2	0	2
Peterson	0	0	0	0
Totals	25	13	35	63

1952 NCAA Tournament
Round 1: Kansas 68, Texas Christian 64
Round 2: Kansas 74, St. Louis 55
Semis: Kansas 74, Santa Clara 55
Finals: Kansas 80, St. Johns 63

1988 NCAA CHAMPIONSHIP

Kansas 83, Oklahoma 79
April 4, 1988 - Kansas City, Mo.

Kansas (83)	M	FG	FT	R	A	TP
*Newton	32	6-6	1-2	4	1	15
*Piper	37	4-6	0-0	7	2	8
*Manning	36	13-24	5-7	18	2	31
*Pritchard	31	6-7	0-0	1	4	13
*Gueldner	15	1-2	0-0	2	1	2
Barry	9	0-2	1-2	0	2	1
Normore	16	3-3	0-1	1	4	7
Harris	13	1-1	0-0	1	0	2
Minor	11	1-4	2-2	1	1	4
Maddox	1	0-0	0-0	0	0	0
Totals	200	35-55	9-14	36	17	83

Oklahoma (79)	M	FG	FT	R	A	TP
*Grant	40	6-14	2-3	5	1	14
*Sieger	40	7-15	1-2	5	7	22
*King	39	7-14	3-3	7	0	17
*Blaylock	40	6-13	0-1	5	4	14
*Grace	34	4-14	3-4	7	5	12
Mullins	4	0-0	0-0	0	0	0
Totals	200	30-70	9-13	31	19	79

*Starters

Halftime Score: Kansas 50, Oklahoma 50
Turnovers: Kansas 23, Oklahoma 15
Shooting Percentages:
FG-Kansas 63.6%Oklahoma 42.9%
FT-Kansas 80.0%Oklahoma 69.2%

Three-Point Goals:
Kansas 4-6 (Newton 2-2, Manning 0-1, Pritchard 1-1, Gueldner 0-1, Normore 1-1)
Oklahoma 10-14 (Sieger 7-13, Blaylock 2-4, Grace 1-7)

1988 NCAA Tournament
Round 1: Kansas 85, Xavier 72
Round 2: Kansas 61, Murray State 58
Round 3: Kansas 66, Vanderbilt 64
Round 4: Kansas 71, Kansas State 58
Semis:Kansas 66, Duke 59
Finals:Kansas 83, Oklahoma 79

INDIVIDUAL NATIONAL HONORS

ALL-AMERICANS
*Consensus first team selections

1909-Tommy Johnson (Lawrence, Kan.)
1915-Ralph Sproull (Lawrence, Kan.)
1919-A.C. Lonborg (Horton, Kan.)
1922-Paul Endacott (Lawrence, Kan.)
1923-Paul Endacott (Lawrence, Kan.)
    Charlie Black (Alton, Ill.)
1924-Tusten Ackerman (Lawrence, Kan.)
    Charlie Black (Alton, Ill.)
1925-Tusten Ackerman (Lawrence, Kan.)
    Gale Gordon (Kansas City, Kan.)
    Albert Peterson (Kansas City, Kan.)
1926-Gale Gordon (Kansas City, Kan.)
    Al Peterson (Kansas City, Kan.)
1930-Forrest Cox (Newton, Kan.)
1932-Ted O'Leary (Lawrence, Kan.)
1933-Bill Johnson (Oklahoma City, Okla.)
1936-Ray Ebling (Lindsborg, Kan.)
1937-Fred Pralle (St. Louis, Mo.)
1938-Fred Pralle (St. Louis, Mo.)*
1941-Howard Engleman (Arkansas City, Kan.)*
1942-Ray Evans (Kansas City, Kan.)
    Charlie Black (Kansas City, Kan.)
1943-Ray Evans (Kansas City, Kan.)
    Charlie Black (Kansas City, Kan.)*
1946-Charlie Black (Kansas City, Kan.)
1947-Charlie Black (Kansas City, Kan.)
1950-Clyde Lovellette (Terre Haute, Ind.)*
1951-Clyde Lovellette (Terre Haute, Ind.)*
1952-Clyde Lovellette (Terre Haute, Ind.)
1953-B.H. Born (Medicine Lodge, Kan.)
1957-Wilt Chamberlain (Philadelphia, Pa.)*
1958-Wilt Chamberlain (Philadelphia, Pa.)*
1961-Bill Bridges (Hobbs, N.M.)
1966-Walt Wesley (Ft. Myers, Fla.)
1968-Jo Jo White (St. Louis, Mo.)
1969-Jo Jo White (St. Louis, Mo.)
1971-Dave Robisch (Springfield, Ill.)
1972-Bud Stallworth (Hartselle, Ala.)
1981-Darnell Valentine (Wichita, Kan.)
1987-Danny Manning (Lawrence, Kan.)*
1988-Danny Manning (Lawrence, Kan.)*

NCAA ALL-TOURNAMENT TEAM
(R-Regional; FF-Final Four)
1940-Howard Engleman (Salina, Kan.), FF.
    Bob Allen (Mission, Kan.), FF.
1952-Clyde Lovellette (Terre Haute, Ind.), R, FF-MVP.
    Dean Kelley (McCune, Kan.), R, FF.
1953-B.H. Born (Medicine Lodge, Kan.), R, FF-MVP.
    Dean Kelley (McCune, Kan.), R, FF.
    Gil Reich (Steelton, Pa.), R.
1957-Wilt Chamberlain (Philadelphia, Pa.), R, FF.
    Maurice King (Kansas City, Kan.), R.
1971-Dave Robisch (Springfield, Ill.), F.
    Bud Stallworth (Hartselle, Ala.), R.
1974-Roger Morningstar (Dundee, Ill.), R.
    Danny Knight (Salina, Kan.), R.
1986-Danny Manning (Lawrence, Kan.), R.
    Calvin Thompson (Kansas City, Kan.), R.
1987-Danny Manning (Lawrence, Kan.), R.
1988-Danny Manning (Lawrence, Kan.), R, FF-MVP.
    Milt Newton (Washington, D.C.), R, FF.

Kevin Pritchard (Tulsa, Okla.), R.
1991-Mark Randall (Englewood, Colo.), FF.
    Alonzo Jamison (Santa Ana, Calif.), R-MVP.
    Adonis Jordan (Reseda, Calif.), R.
    Terry Brown (Clyde, N.Y.), R.

ACADEMIC ALL-AMERICANS
1971-Bud Stallworth (Hartselle, Ala.)
1974-Tom Kivisto (Aurora, Ill.)
1977-Chris Barnthouse (Winfield, Kan.)
    Ken Koenigs (Goddard, Kan.)
1978-Ken Koenigs (Goddard, Kan.)
1979-Darnell Valentine (Wichita, Kan.)
1980-Darnell Valentine (Wichita, Kan.)
1981-Darnell Valentine (Wichita, Kan.)
1982-David Magley (South Bend, Ind.)

NATIONAL COLLEGIATE PLAYER-OF-THE-YEAR
1923-Paul Endacott (Lawrence, Kan.) - Helms Foundation
1924-Charlie Black (Alton, Ill.) - Helms Foundation
1952-Clyde Lovellette (Terre Haute, Ind.) - Helms Foundation
1988-Danny Manning (Lawrence, Kan.) - Kodak, Naismith, Wooden

NATIONAL COACHING HONORS
1978-Ted Owens (National Coach-of-the-Year/Basketball Weekly)
1988-Larry Brown (National Coach-of-the-Year/Naismith Foundation)
1989-Roy Williams (National Coach-of-the-Year/Basketball Times)
1990-Roy Williams (National Coach-of-the-Year/USBWA) (National Coach of the Year/Moulton, Billy Packer)
1991-Roy Williams (National Coach of the Year/L.A. Times)
1992-Roy Williams (Naitonal Coach of the Year/Associated Press)

NCAA POST-GRADUATE AWARDS
1974-Tom Kivisto (Aurora, Ill.)
1978-Ken Koenigs (Goddard, Kan.)

OLYMPIC TEAM MEMBERS
1952 at Helsinki-Clyde Lovellette (Terre Haute, Ind.), Bill Lienhard (Newton, Kan.), John Keller (Page City, Kan.), Bob Kenney (Winfield, Kan.), Dean Kelley (McCune, Kan.), Bill Hougland (Beloit, Kan.), Charlie Hoag (Oak Park, Ill.), Dr. F.C. Allen (assistant coach)
1956 at Melbourne-Bill Hougland (Beloit, Kan.)
1960 at Rome-Allen Kelley (McCune, Kan.), Dean Nesmith (team trainer), A.C. Lonborg (team manager)
1968 at Mexico City-Jo Jo White (St. Louis, Mo.)
1980 (boycott)-Darnell Valentine (Wichita, Kan.)
1988 at Seoul-Danny Manning (Lawrence, Kan.)

MOST OUTSTANDING PLAYER NCAA TOURNAMENT
1952-Clyde Lovellette (Terre Haute, Ind.)
1953-B.H. Born (Medicine Lodge, Kan.)
1957-Wilt Chamberlain (Philadelphia, Pa.)
1988-Danny Manning (Lawrence, Kan.)

ALL-CONFERENCE SELECTIONS

*First Team Selections Only

MISSOURI VALLEY

1911-Verne Long, Bob Heizer, Don Dousman
1913-C.R. Greenlees
1915-Ralph Sproull, Ephriam Sorensen, Art Weaver,
　　Stuffy Dunmire
1919-Dutch Lonborg
1920-Dutch Lonborg
1922-George Rody, Paul Endacott
1923-John Wulf, Paul Endacott, Charlie Black
1924-Tusten Ackerman, Charlie Black, Bob Mosby
1925-Tusten Ackerman, Al Peterson
1926-Gale Gordon, Al Peterson
1927-Al Peterson, Glenn Burton

BIG SIX

1930-Tom Bishop, Frosty Cox
1931-Tom Bishop, Frosty Cox
1932-Ted O'Leary, Bill Johnson, Lee Page
1933-Bill Johnson
1934-Ray Ebling
1935-Dick Wells, Ray Ebling
1936-Ray Ebling, Francis Kappelman, Fred Pralle
1937-Fred Pralle
1938-Fred Pralle
1939-Lyman Corlis
1940-Ralph Miller, Bob Allen, Howard Engleman
1941-Howard Engleman, Bob Allen
1942-Ralph Miller, Charlie Black, Ray Evans
1943-Otto Schnellbacher, Ray Evans, John Buescher,
　　Charlie Black
1945-Gordon Reynolds, Kirk Scott
1946-Charlie Black, Otto Schnellbacher
1947-Charlie Black, Otto Schnellbacher

BIG SEVEN

1948-Otto Schnellbacher
1950-Clyde Lovellette
1951-Clyde Lovellette
1952-Clyde Lovellette, Bob Kenney
1953-B.H. Born, Al Kelley
1954-B.H. Born, Al Kelley, Harold Patterson, Dallas
　　Dobbs
1955-Dallas Dobbs
1956-Maurice King
1957-Wilt Chamberlain, Gene Elstun
1958-Wilt Chamberlain, Ron Loneski

BIG EIGHT

1959-Bill Bridges
1960-Bill Bridges, Wayne Hightower
1961-Bill Bridges, Wayne Hightower
1962-Jerry Gardner, Nolen Ellison
1963-Nolen Ellison
1964-George Unseld
1965-Walter Wesley
1966-Walter Wesley, Del Lewis
1967-Jo Jo White, Rodger Bohnenstiehl
1968-Jo Jo White
1969-Jo Jo White. Dave Robisch
1970-Dave Robisch
1971-Dave Robisch, Bud Stallworth
1972-Bud Stallworth

1974-Tom Kivisto
1975-Rick Suttle
1976-Norman Cook
1977-John Douglas
1978-Ken Koenigs, Darnell Valentine
1979-Darnell Valentine
1980-Darnell Valentine
1981-Darnell Valentine
1982-David Magley
1984-Carl Henry
1985-Ron Kellogg
1986-Danny Manning, Ron Kellogg
1987-Danny Manning
1988-Danny Manning
1990-Kevin Pritchard
1991-Mark Randall
1992-Adonis Jordan, Rex Walters
1993-Rex Walters

BIG EIGHT NEWCOMER-OF-THE-YEAR

1967-Vernon Vanoy
1977-John Douglas
1978-Darnell Valentine
1985-Danny Manning
1990-Rick Calloway (Co-Newcomer-of-the-year)
1992-Rex Walters

BIG EIGHT PLAYER-OF-THE-YEAR

1970-Dave Robisch
1971-Dave Robisch
1972-Bud Stallworth
1986-Danny Manning
1987-Danny Manning
1988-Danny Manning

BIG EIGHT COACH-OF-THE-YEAR

1966-Ted Owens
1967-Ted Owens
1971-Ted Owens
1974-Ted Owens
1978-Ted Owens
1986-Larry Brown
1990-Roy Williams
1992-Roy Williams

ACADEMIC ALL-BIG EIGHT

1973-Tom Kivisto
1974-Tom Kivisto, Dale Greenlee
1975-Dale Greenlee
1976-Cris Barnthouse, Ken Koenigs
1977-Cris Barnthouse, Ken Koenigs
1978-Ken Koenigs
1979-Darnell Valentine
1980-Darnell Valentine
1981-Darnell Valentine
1982-Tony Guy, David Magley
1983-Jeff Dishman
1986-Mark Turgeon
1988-Chris Piper, Kevin Pritchard
1989-Kevin Pritchard
1990-Kevin Pritchard, Mark Randall
1991-Mark Randall, Mike Maddox
1992- David Johanning

KANSAS ALL-TIME LETTERMEN

* Denotes Captain of team

A Ackerman, Arthur*, C, F, 1923-25; Adams, Ira*, G, F, 1904-05; Adams, Irwin*, F, G, 1903-04; Alberts, Jerry, F, 1953-54; Alexander, Todd, G, 1990; Alford, Donald, F, C, 1902-03; Alford, Joseph*, F, C, 1901-04; Allen, Forrest C., C, F, 1905-07; Allen, Harry, C, 1902-04; Allen, Milton, F, G, 1934-36; Allen, Robert*, C, 1939-41; Allphin, Clyde, 1900-03; Alvarado, Sean, C, 1987, 1989; Ames, Loren, 1903; Anderson, Ferrel, 1937-38; Anderson, John*, G,

1953-55; Anderson, Robert, 1946; Anderson, Scott, F, 1977-78; Appel, Hilmar, F, G, 1915-16; Arndt, Howard, F, 1967-69; Arnold, James, 1941; Atkinson, Paul, C, 1902; Auten, Don, 1946-47; Avery, Herbert, G, 1899

B Baker, Hoyt, 1943, 1946; Baker, Ralph, G, 1931; Ballard, John, G, 1942-43, 1946; Ballard, Eugene, 1946, 1948; Banks, Tim, G, 1983-84; Barlow, Frank, F, G, 1904-06; Barnthouse, Chris, G, 1975-77; Barr,

Eugene, 1946, 1948; Barrington, Donald, F, 1944; Barrow, Wilson*, F, 1972-73; Barry, Richard (Scooter)*, G, 1986-89; Bausch, Frank, G, 1930, 1932; Bausch, James, 1930; Beck, Walter, G, 1951; Belgard, Wilferd*, G, 1924-26; Benn, Carl, 1933; Bennett, Roy, G, F, 1919-21; Bergen, Ralph, C, G, 1906-09; Bernhard, Bernice, manager, 1902; Billings, Robert, G, 1957-59; Bishop, Tom*, F, 1929-31; Black, Charles B.*, F, 1942-43, 1946-47; Black, Charles T.*, G, F, 1922-24; Blair, Donald, G, 1942-43; Bliss, Charles*, F, 1905; Boagni, Kerry, F, 1983; Boehm, Walter, C, 1912-13; Bohnenstiehl, Roger*, F, 1966-68; Bolton, Kerry, G, 1963-65; Born, B.H.*, C, 1952-54; Bosilevac, Fred, F, 1937; Bosilevac, Fred Jr., F, 1970-72; Bowman, Waldo, F, 1922-23; Boyle, Thomas (Tad)*, G, 1982-85; Bradshaw, Richard, G, 1969; Brainard, William, 1954-56; Branch, Marvin, C, 1988; Bridges, Bill, F, 1959-61; Brill, David, F, 1963-65; Brill, William, 1943; Brown, Andrew, G, 1902-04; Brown, Loren, 1912-13; Brown, Roger, C, 1969-71; Brown, Terry*, G, 1990-91; Buescher, John*, C, 1941-43; Bukaty, Frank, 1939; Bull, Clinton, F, G, 1949-51; Buller, Kenneth, F, 1953; Bunn, John, G, F, 1918-20; Burton, Glenn*, G, 1926-28

C Calloway, Rick*, F, 1990; Campbell, Altonio, G, 1985-86; Campbell, Clifford, F, 1925-26; Canfield, Randy, G, 1971-72; Carlson, Norman, F, 1945; Carroll, William, F, G, 1979-80; Chamberlain, Wilton, C, 1957-58; Chana, Fred, F, 1964-66; Clark, Wendell, G, 1946-47; Cleland, John, G, 1956-58; Cole, Lawrence*, C, 1914-16; Cook, Arthur, C, 1904; Cook, Norman*, F, 1974-76; Corder, Dean, C, 1944-46; Corlis, Lyman*, G, F, 1937-39; Correll, Allen*, F, 1960-61, 1963-64; Cox, Forrest*, G, 1929-31; Cox, Marvin, G, F, 1936; Crawford, John, F, 1978-81; Crosswhite, William, F, G, 1926; Curd, Robert, F, 1934; Czaplinski, Lane*, G, 1992

D Daniels, John, F, C, 1926; Dater, Edwin, G, 1956-57; Daum, Gustave, G, C, 1945-46; Davenport, Lawrence, 1952-55; Davis, Ben, F, 1992; Davis, Patrick, G, 1966-67; Deane, Carl, G, 1962; Dennis, David, F, 1949; Dewell, John, G, 1948; Dick, George, G, 1942-44; Diehl, Donald, G, 1944; Dishman, Jeffery, F, 1982-83; Dixon, Armand, G, 1943; Dobbs, Dallas*, G, 1954-56; Dodd, Leo, C, 1928-29; Donaghue, Alan, F, 1958-60; Douglas, Greg, F, 1968, 1971; Douglas, John*, G, 1977-78; Douglas, Keith, G, 1980; Dousman, Donald*, F, G, 1911-12; Dreiling, Greg*, C, 1984-86; Dumas, Jimmy*, F, 1961-63; Dunmire, Ray*, G, 1913-15; Durand, Fenlon, F, 1937-38; Dye, Everett, F, G, 1953

E Ebling, Donald*, F, 1938-40; Ebling, Ray*, F, 1934-36; Ediger, Jaye, F, 1967; Ellison, Benoyd, F, G, 1960-61; Ellison, Nolen*, 1961-63; Elstun, Donald*, G, 1955-57; Doug Elstun, G, 1991; Emley, Samuel, C, 1899; Endacott, Paul*, G, 1921-23; Engel, Dale, 1949-51; Engel, Verne, F, 1924-25; England, Harold, F, 1947-50; Engleman, Howard*, 1939-41; Enns, Myron, F, G, 1948, 1951; Eskridge, Jack, G, 1947-48; Evans, Ray, G, 1942-43, 1946-47; Ewing, Mark, C, 1982-83

F Fearing, Olin, F, 1918-20; Fees, Charles, G, 1901-02; Fiddelke, Michael, F, 1973; Filkin, Lawrence, F, 1933; Fitzpatrick, Wilson, 1942-43; Flachsbarth, Leland, C, 1962; Florell, Loren, F, 1938-39; Folks, Ray, G, 1914-16; Forsyth, William, 1943; Fowler, Wilmore, G 1978-79; Frank, Willard, F, 1944; Franklin, Kenneth, G, 1972; Franz, Ronald, F, 1965-67; Frederick, Byron, C, 1919, 1922-23; Frisby, Donald, G, 1946

G Gardner, Jerry, G, 1960-62; Gear, George, 1946; Gibbens, Leon, 1916-17; Gibson, Harry*, F, 1962-64; Gibson, MIlton, G, 1975-78; Giles, Chester, C, F,

1979-80; Gisel, Richard, G, 1960; Goehring, Louis, G, C, 1944-45; Golay, George, F, 1937-38; Gordon, Gale, C, 1925-27; Gough, James, F, 1964-65; Gray, Gordon, G, 1933-35; Green, Leland, F, 1955-57; Greenlee, Dale*, G, 1973-75; Greenlees, Charles*, F, 1912-14; Griggs, Adessie, F, 1904; Gueldner, Jeff*, G, 1987-90; Guiot, Jeffery, G, 1983-84; Gurley, Greg, G, 1992-93; Guy, Anthony*, G, 1979-82

H Haase, Dale, F, 1972-73; Hacket, John, C, 1908; Hall, Edward, 1941; Hall, Vance, F, 1941-42; Hancock, Darrin, 1993; Harmon, Phillip, 1967-69; Harms, Marvin, 1919-20; Harp, Richard*, G, 1938-40; Harrington, Paul*, F, 1932-34; Harris, Fred, 1934; Harris, Keith, F, 1987-88; Hauser, Harold, C, 1928; Heckert, Henry, C, 1924; Heim, Herbert, G, C, 1945; Heitholt, Arthur, 1952-54; Heizer, Robert*, C, 1909-11; Henderson, Willis, G, 1898-99; Henry, Carl*, G, 1983-84; Hess, Henry, 1899; Hess, William, F, C, 1898; Heyward, Ralph, F, 1961; Hickman, Robert, G, 1958-60; Hicks, Albert, C, F, 1902-04; Hightower, Wayne, F, 1960-61; Hill, Everett, G, 1945; Hill, James*, F, 1926-28; Hill, Lance, G, 1982-83; Hite, Ora, F, 1912-13; Hitt, Ward, G, F, 1926; Hoag, Charlie, G, 1951-52; Hodges, Gregory, G, F, 1926; Hoffman, James, F, 1958-60; Hogben, William, G, 1940; Holliday, James, 1936-37; Hollinger, Blaine, G, 1955-57; Holmer, Robert, 1936; Houchin, Claude*, G, 1947-50; Hougland, William, F, G, 1950-52; Houk, Clarence, F, 1921; House, Jerry, F, 1971-72; Housey, Arthur, C, 1980-81; Hoyt, Harold, 1899; Hull, Rodney, F, 1985-86; Hunt, Robert, 1938; Hunter, Cedric, G, 1984-87; Hunter, Thomas, G, 1940-42

I Israel, Warren, F, 1942

J Jamison, Alonzo*, F, 1990-92; Jeffrey, Balfour, G, 1927-28; Jennings, Charles, 1902; Jett, Harry, F, 1956-57; Johanning, David*, C, 1991-92; Johnson, Carl, G, 1938; Johnson, Charles, 1906; Johnson, Clinton, G, 1975-78; Johnson, Jeff, G, 1985-86; Johnson, Jerry, 1958; Johnson, Jerry L., F, 1986; Johnson, Lewis, C, 1955-57; Johnson, Monte, F, 1957-59; Johnson, Tholmas*, F, 1909-11; Johnson, Wallace, 1940-42; Johnson, William*, 1931-33; Johnston, Ronald, G, 1955-57; Jordan, Adonis*, G, 1990-93

K Kaiser, Karl, G, C, 1915; Kampschroeder, Brad, F, 1989; Kappelman, Francis, G, 1934-36; Kappelman, Lester, G, F, 1937-39; Kauder, Walter, F, G, 1916-17; Keller, John, F, G, 1951-52; Kelley, Earl*, G, 1953-54; Kelley, Melvin*, G, 1951-53; Kellogg, Ronald, F, G, 1983-86; Kennedy, Carl, F, 1916; Kenney, Robert, 1950-52; Ketchum, Dee, 1959-61; Kindred, Lynn, G, 1957-59; King, Clifford, 1974; King, Maurice, F, 1955-57; Kissell, Max, F, C, 1942-43; Kivisto, Robert, G, 1970-71; Kivisto, Thomas*, G, 1972-74; Klaas, Roy, G, 1933; Kline, John*, F, G, 1939-41; Knight, Danny*, C, 1973-75; Knight, Kelly*, F, C, 1980, 1982-84; Knight, Mark, G, F, 1981; Knoles, James, F, 1918; Koenigs, Kenneth*, C, 1975-78; Konek, Jeffrey, G, 1981

L Larson, Harold, G, 1910-11; Larson, Louis, G, 1908; Laslett, Howard*, G, 1917, 1919; Lattin, Clarence, G, 1926-27; Lawrence, William*, G, 1968-70; Lewis, Delvin*, G, 1964-66; Lienhard, William, 1950-52; Lindsey, Adrian, 1917; Linquist, William, 1944; Linville, Aubrey, G, 1950; Lochmann, Riney*, F, 1964-66; Lockley, Robert, F, 1956; Lonborg, Arthur*, 1918-20; Lonborg, John, 1922-24; Loneski, Ronald, G, 1957-59; Long, Verne, F, 1909-11; Lopes, Albert, G, F, 1965-66; Lovellette, Clyde*, C, 1950-52; Loving, Wayne, G, 1964; Lutton, Lyle, G, 1937; Lytle, Harold, G, 1916-17

Mc McCauley, James, G, 1904; McCormick, George,

G, 1929; McCune, George*, F, 1907-09; McDonald, Andrew, F, 1921-23; McElroy, Harold, F, 1954; McGuire, Clarence, 1928-29; McSpadden, Harold*, G, 1943-44

M Mabry, Guy, F, 1948-50; Maddox, Mike*, F, 1988-91; Magley, David*, F, 1979-82; Malott, Robert, F, 1944; Mandeville, Frank, G, 1918; Maney, Robert, G, 1927-29; Manning, Danny*, F, 1985-88; Markkanen, Pekka, G, 1990; Marshall, Archie*, F, 1986, 1988; Marshall, Grover, G, 1961; Marshall, Mike, G, 1984; Martin, Brian*, C, 1982-84; Martin, Maurice, 1946, 1948-49; Martindell, Donald, G, 1908-10; Mask, Neal, F, 1970-72; Mason, Edward, G, 1919; Mathews, Kelsey*, C, 1918-19; Mathews, Mark, F, 1970-72; Matt, John, C, 1961-63; Mattox, Marvin, F, 1988; Michaelson, Manley, F, 1904; Miller, Howard, F, 1918-20; Miller, Milton*, G, 1905-08; Miller, Richard, 1942; Miller, William, C, 1905-08; Minor, Lincoln, G, 1988-89; Mitchell, Victor, C, 1981; Moffett, Charles, F, C, 1944-45, 1949; Mokeski, Paul*, G, 1976-79; Morningstar, Roger, F, 1974-75; Mosby, James, G, 1923

N Nash, Aubrey, G, 1970-72; Nash, David, 1968-69; Nash, Macolm*, F, 1990-92; Natsus, Timothy, G, 1969; Neal, Douglas, G 1978-81; Nees, Charles, G, 1938-39; Nelson, Lawrence*, G, 1916-17; Newland, Carmen, F, 1927-28; Newton, Milt*, F, 1985, 1987-89; Nicholson, Eldon, 1953; Noble, Raymond*, G, F, 1935-37; Nobles, Herbert, F, 1976-77; Normore, Clint, G, 1988

O O'Leary, Thedore*, F, 1930-32; Olson, Herbert, C, 1920-21; Ostertag, Greg, C, 1992-93; Owen, Arthur, G, 1938; Owens, Eugene, F, C, 1898-1901; Owens, Frederick*, G, F, 1898-1902; Oyler, Robert, 1934-35

P Padgett, Gary, F, 1954-55; Page, Leland*, G, 1930-32; Parker, John*, G, 1955-57; Pauley, Eric*, C, 1992-93; Patterson, Harold, F, 1953-54; Pattinson, Darwin, G, 1916; Peacock, Charles, G, 1982; Peard, Roger, F, 1908; Pearson, Sean, 1993; Peck, Owen, C, F, 1945-47; Pellock, Mark, F, 1985, 1987; Penny, Charles, F, 1947-49; Petersen, Albert, C, 1925-27; Peterson, Arthur, 1946, 49-50; Piatt, William, 1904; Piper, Chris*, F, 1985-88; Plumley, Francis, F, 1929; Pooler, Arthur, 1903-04; Pralle, Ferdinand*, G, 1936-38; Priest, Richard, 1904; Pritchard, Kevin*, G, 1987-90; Proudfit, Herbert, F, 1926

Q Queens, Eugene, 1898

R Ramsey, Floyd, G, 1929-31; Randall, Mark*, C, F, 1987, 1989-91; Rayford, Calvin, 1993; Reber, John, 1916; Reich, Gilbert, G, 1953; Reid, Bruce, F, C, 1938; Renko, Steve, F, 1964; Replogle, Max, G, 1939; Reynolds, Albert, 1945; Rice, Carl, G, 1918; Richey, Patrick, G, F, 1991-93; Roberts, Jay, F, 1962-63; Robisch, David, F, 1969-71; Rody, George*, F, 1920-22; Rogers, Marshall, 1973; Rogers, Paul*, F, 1935-37; Ross, Ricky, G, 1980; Rouse, Carl, freshman coach, 1909; Royal, Claude, 1899-1900; Ruggles, Richard, G, 1964; Rupp, Adolph, C, G, 1923; Russell, Pierre*, F, 1969-71; Russell, Rusel, G, 1899-1900

S Samuel, Nino, F, 1973; Sanders, Bradford*, G,

1976-79; Sands, Jack, C, 1939-40; Sanneman, Norman, C, 1941; Sapp, Ora*, G, 1947-49; Schaake, Elmer, G, 1932-33; Schaake, William, 1951; Schichtle, David*, G, 1963-65; Schmidt, George*, F, 1925-27; Schmidt, Sylvester*, F, 1937-38; Schnellbacher, Otto*, F, 1943, 46-48; Scott, Closson, G, 1945; Scott, Richard, F, 1991-93; Shaffer, Wilmer, F, 1934-36; Sherwood, Homer, C, 1944; Short, John, F, 1943; Siler, Charles, F, C, 1905-07; Sloan, Bruce*, G, 1967-69; Smith, Cecil, 1906; Smith, Chester*, G, 1901-02; Smith, Dean, F, 1952-53; Smith, Lester, G, 1912-13; Smith, Lynwood, 1949-50; Smith, Tommie, F, 1973-75; Smith, Verni, G, 1910; Snow, Mark, C, 1980; Snyder, Harry, G, 1910-12; Sollenberger, Marvin, G, 1941-42; Sorensen, Ephraim, F, 1915; Sparks, Loye, F, 1962-63; Sproull, Ralph*, F, 1913-15; Squires, La Vannes, 1953-54; Stallcup, John (Mac)*, F, 1978-80; Stallworth, Isaac (Bud)*, F, 1970-72; Stramel, Gilbert, F, 1946-48; Stratton, Daniel, 1924; Stucker, Charles, 1944; Stuckey, George, F, 1911-12; Sullivan, Nelson, F, 1938; Summers, Mark*, F, 1981-83; Suttle, Richard, F, 1973-75; Sutton, Walter, 1899; Sutton, William*, 1899

T Taynor, David*, G, 1972-74; Thomas, Richard, G, 1967-68; Thompson, Calvin, F, 1983-86; Thompson, Gary, F, 1957-59; Thompson, George, F, 1981; Thomson, Charles*, 1928-30; Toft, James, 1956; Tolan, John, G, 1902; Turgeon, Mark*, G, 1984-87; Turner, Jesse, F, 1942-43; Turner, Robert, 1944; Tunstall, Sean, G, 1991

U Uhrlaub, Ernst*, F, G, 1917, 1919-21; Uhrlaub, Rudolf*, G, F, 1916-18; Ulrich, Hubert, 1942; Unseld, George, C, 1963-64; Urie, Raymond, 1933

V Vance, Robert, G, 1962-64; Valentine, Darnell*, G, 1978-81; Van der Vries, Edward, F, 1910, 1914; Vanek, Ernst, G, 1932, 1934; Vanoy, Vernon, C, 1967-68; Von Moore, Donnie, F, C, 1975, 1977-78; Voran, Bruce, C, G, 1939-40

W Wagner, Kirk*, F, 1990-91; Walker, Charles, G, C, 1941-42; Walters, Rex*, G, 1992-93; Watson, Raymond, F, 1910; Waugh, Gerald*, C, 1948-51; Weaver, Arthur, C, 1912-14; Weichbroot, Blake, 1993; Weidlein, William, G, 1914; Weidner, Carl, G, 1937; Welch, Mark, G, 1981; Wellhausen, Al, C, 1935, 1937; Wells, Dick*, F, C, 1933-35; Wells, Marion, G, F, 1950-51; Wesley, Walter, C, 1964-66; West, Freeman*, F, 1989-90; Whatley, TJ, 1993; White, Joseph*, G, 1966-69; Whitfield, Claude, F, 1928-29; Weinecke, Edwin, 1938; Wilkin, William, F, G, 1923, 1925; Williams, Edgar, F, 1945; Wilson, Robert, G, 1966; Winnagle, Roscoe, G, F, 1905-06; Woestemeyer, Armin, F, 1921-23; Wohler, Paul, 1907-08; Wolfe, Jack, G, 1954; Woodberry, Steve, G, 1991-93; Woodward, Brinton, G, 1962; Woodward, Earl*, G, 1907-10; Woodward, George, 1917; Worrel, Richard, F, 1981; Wulf, John, C, 1921-23

Y Yahn, William, 1899-1900; Yarnevich, George, F, 1967

Z Zuber, Harold, C, F, 1925-27

TRIVIA ANSWERS

1. Naismith was born in Almonte, Canada, on Nov. 6, 1861. He moved to the United States in 1890.

2. KU first played Nebraska on March 2, 1900. The Jayhawks lost 48-8 at Lincoln.

3. Will Sutton, who scored the Jayhawks' first points ever with his foul shot against the Kansas City YMCA, was the captain of the first team.

4. Getting basketball started at KU was a somewhat complicated process. According to the 1899 Oread, teams for each class level were formed, in addition to teams from the engineering, law and pharmacy schools. Even the faculty got in on the act, forming a team that by all accounts was fairly competitive. The sophomores prevailed in this inter-class format, and a team was chosen from the best players on each team "to represent the University against all comers."

5. KU's first home court in the basement of Snow featured support pillars scattered throughout the court and an 11-foot ceiling until the floor was lowered to

give a 16-foot clearance. Opponents eventually refused to risk playing there and the Jayhawks spent a lot of time on the road in the early years.

6. Robinson, located where Wescoe Hall now stands, cost $100,000 to build.

7. The gym would seat 3,000 frenzied Jayhawk fans.

8. It was named for Gov. Charles Robinson and his wife, Sara, who donated the land on which it was built.

9. Forward George McCune was captain of the 1907-08 MVC championship team.

10. Track

11. KU All-American Ralph "Lefty" Sproull

12. Missouri Coach Van Ghent had travelled to Lawrence to see the game — the first report of "scouting" an opponent. Hamilton, in turn, travelled to Manhattan to watch Missouri beat K-State the next week. KU and MU split their season-ending series.

13. Emporia Normal beat the Jayhawks 36-25 in Lawrence on Feb. 24, 1916. The "Teacher five" were coached by Bill Hargiss, a former Hamilton assistant at KU.

14. As an assistant basketball coach.

15. It was the first time in 13 years of the KU-MU series that the Tigers had won a game in Lawrence.

16. Phog Allen, still coaching at Warrensburg, chose the team. He was qualified to do so, the conference decided, since he had officiated many MVC games. Allen didn't name a single Jayhawk to the first team and wouldn't even consider Scrubby Laslett because "he played his man too closely."

17. Team captain Rudolf Uhrlaub also went by "Dutch."

18. Allen was a baseball umpire and when he made his calls, his voice was said to sound like a foghorn. A sportswriter later changed the spelling to "Phog" and it stuck.

19. His players and friends always referred to him as "Doc," a reference to work as an osteopath.

20. Paul Endacott, in 1921, '22 and '23.

21. The starting five of the 1942-43 team that went 10-0 and won the Big Six title: Charlie Black, John Buescher, Ray Evans, Otto Schnellbacher and Armand Dixon.

22. The Opera House

23. Charlie Black the Second. He went to the Anderson Packers in the NBL in 1947 and joined the NBA Ft. Wayne Pistons in 1948. He also played with the Indianapolis Jets and Milwaukee Hawks before wrapping up his pro career in 1952.

24. The Chanute Comet. At Chanute (Kan.) High School, the multisport talent had earned letters in football (4), basketball (3), track (4), golf (1) and tennis (1).

25. B.H.Born, the Lonesome Pine from Medicine Lodge was the first member of a non-title team to be named the tournament MVP.

26. "Smiles"

27. Dick Harp also served as color commentator on KU football broadcasts, one season winning a state broadcasting award for his work.

28. He dubbed the home "Ursa Major," which means Big Dipper, his favorite nickname.

29. Bill Bridges, with 1,081, is second in career rebounding, behind Danny Manning's 1,187.

30. In the 1972-73 season, KU went 8-18 under Ted Owens.

31. The losing seasons in 1962 and 1963 were the first back-to-back since James Naismith was the Jayhawk coach in 1903-04, 1904-05.

32. "Teddy," as his coach at OU, Bruce Drake, called him, "was one of the greatest two-handed set shots that I have ever seen in basketball." Owens practiced that set shot relentlessly, wearing out two or three basketballs every summer, Drake said when Owens was first hired at KU.

33. With a 9-5 record in the Big Eight, KU finished second and Owens became the first Jayhawks coach not to win a conference title in his first season at KU. (With the exception of Naismith. The Jayhawks were not members of a conference during his tenure.)

34. Accounts vary. Media guides from his time at KU say Jo Jo was given the nickname of the major-league outfielder Jo Jo White, who played in his hometown of St. Louis. Another account said it came from his high school coach, who always had to yell his name twice to get his attention.

35. He was the first to play both football and basketball. Vanoy was named Sophomore of the Year in the Big Eight for basketball and was a starting defensive end for Pepper Rodgers' first KU football team.

36. Gary Bender, who received his master's degree in radio and television at KU in 1964, was the play-by-play announcer for KU for two seasons before moving on to Madison, Wisc.

37. Bob Marcum, who resigned as AD to go to South Carolina; Jim Lessig, who was AD for a couple of months before becoming commissioner of the Mid-American Conference; and Monte Johnson, who replaced Lessig.

38. In his KU career, Larry Brown never won at Iowa State, going 0-5 in Ames.

39. He picked up the name in elementary school. His father's name was Horace, but the kids thought it was "Horse," and started calling Calvin "Pony."

40. The Jayhawks won at Detroit (60-51) and at Oklahoma State (85-69) while wearing red.

41. All four had taken teams to NCAA title games: Jim Valvano (N.C. State, 1983); Jud Heathcote (Michigan State, 1979); Johnny Orr (Michigan, 1976); and Larry Brown (UCLA, 1980).

42. Clint Normore and Marvin Mattox were both members of KU's football team.

43. Adonis Jordan.

44. Louisville in 1991-92 and Long Beach State in 1992-93.

45. One, during the first half of the 1991 NCAA final against Duke.

46. Alonzo Jamison had eight steals in a game twice during his career at KU. Zo set the mark during home games against Marquette on Dec. 1, 1990, and against Pepperdine on Jan. 2, 1992.

47. They both scored 1,000 points or more in only two seasons of play. The only other two KU players to achieve that were Wayne Hightower and Carl Henry.

48. No. 8 Charles T. Black, No. 10 Charles B. Black, No. 12 Paul Endacott, No. 16 Clyde Lovellette, No. 23 B.H. Born, No. 25 Danny Manning and No. 31 Lynette Woodard. Wilt Chamberlain's jersey (No. 13) is waiting to join the others in the Allen Fieldhouse rafters when arrangements are made for him to return to Lawrence for a ceremony.

49. Mark Randall, Danny Manning, Dave Robisch, Clyde Lovellette and Wilt Chamberlain.